"A stunningly moving odyssey through modern Buddhist Asia, filled with voluptuous decadence, oceans of tears, ancient cultures, and ravaged hearts. *Hard Travel* takes us into the mouths of the demons who guard the temples and leaves us in the wise and merciful heart of the Buddha."

—JACK KORNFIELD, author of A PATH WITH HEART

"Every scene, every word is underlined and meaningful, from the point of view of grief. Like morphine withdrawal, grief sensitizes the observer, since it cannot be denied. *He is held right there.* And like the Ancient Mariner, Wurlitzer holds his reader right there by his account."

—WILLIAM S. BURROUGHS, author of NAKED LUNCH

"A book to be read on many levels: as a traveler's tale, as a map of grief, as an inspiring record of the stations of the soul."

—GITA MEHTA, author of RAJ and RIVER SUTRA

"A beautifully written, deeply rewarding, intensely affecting work . . . asking extraordinarily hard questions, well-asked and well worth consideration. . . . Luminous, gripping, and spare, it offers a breathtakingly naked glimpse into the life of a man and society at the very edge. Can there be any more gracious gift than that?"

—CHRIS FAATZ, SUNDAY OREGONIAN

"Being as I am far more accustomed to hard travel than to sacred places, it is a real testament to the talent and intelligence of Rudolph Wurlitzer that he completely won me over with this insightful and moving book."

—FRAN LEBOWITZ, author of METROPOLITAN LIFE

"A brave, unsparingly candid exploration of a spiritual relationship between East and West, written by a voyager of the heart with few illusions but real faith."

   —ANDREW HARVEY, author of <u>HIDDEN JOURNEY</u>

"This is a book about going away to the most exotic corners in the world and seeing the phantasmagoria of our modern life, and it is also about discovering that to go away, no matter how far, is inevitably a journey into oneself. Wurlitzer returns with images that will stir and haunt his readers for many years."

   —LEONARD MICHAELS, author of <u>SYLVIA</u>

"A veracious and heartbreaking account of our modern spiritual dilemma. Rudolph Wurlitzer cuts straight to the bone and never spares himself in the process."

   —SAM SHEPARD, author of <u>FOOL FOR LOVE</u>

"A grave and compelling book. Balanced against an aggregate of stern and lovely Buddhist esoterica is a sweaty, personal, hopeless journey through modern Thailand, Burma, and Cambodia. It fulfills itself down to the last empty drop."

   —JOY WILLIAMS, author of <u>STATE OF GRACE</u> and <u>ESCAPES</u>

"As *Hard Travel to Sacred Places* so effectively demonstrates, living at ease with truths is not a graceful process. . . . This book is ultimately successful as an honest description of the hard travel of a soul through a grief-filled world."

   —JOSEPH BEDNARIK, <u>TONIC</u> (Portland, Oregon)

hard travel
to sacred places

Rudolph Wurlitzer

hard travel
to sacred places

SHAMBHALA
Boston & London
1995

Shambhala Publications, Inc.
Horticultural Hall
300 Massachusetts Avenue
Boston, Massachusetts 02115

9   8   7   6   5   4   3   2   1

First Paperback Edition
Printed in the United States of America on acid-free paper ⊗
Distributed in the United States by Random House, Inc.,
and in Canada by Random House of Canada Ltd

   The Library of Congress catalogues the hardcover edition
   of this book as follows:
Wurlitzer, Rudolph.
     Hard travel to sacred places/Rudolph Wurlitzer.
         —1st ed.   p.   cm.
   ISBN 1-57062-024-5 (alk. paper)
   ISBN 1-57062-117-9 (pbk.)
     1. Cambodia—Description and travel.   2. Thailand
   —Description and travel.   3. Burma—Description and
   travel.   4. Buddhism—Cambodia.   5. Buddhism—
   Thailand.   6. Buddhism—Burma.   7. Wurlitzer, Rudolph
   —Journeys—Cambodia.   8. Wurlitzer, Rudolph—Journeys—
   Thailand.   9. Wurlitzer, Rudolph—Journeys—Burma.   I. Title.
   DS554.382.W87   1994   94-6195
   915.9—dc20   CIP

contents

thailand

TUESDAY, MARCH 15, 1993. After a twenty-two-hour flight from L.A., the Bangkok airport feels like a hi-tech pit stop in an endless *bardo* tunnel, that strange in-between state that the Buddhists believe exists between life and death. Dazed and wrecked, my wife, Lynn Davis, and I stumble through customs, only to be met unexpectedly by Prince Chatri, a member of the royal family. He had been notified of our arrival by an English-Italian movie producer who had asked me to direct a script I had written from one of my novels, *Slow Fade*. In the time-honored tradition of the Italian film industry, the producer had failed to show up to scout locations but at the last minute had provided Chatri as a substitute (an amazing gift, as it turned out). I had completely forgotten about this "film" plan, as we had been concentrating on Lynn's assignment from a New York magazine to photograph the sacred Buddhist sites of Thailand, Burma, and Cambodia.

And then I remember the real reason we have come.

Six months ago Lynn's twenty-one-year-old son, Ayrev, was killed in a car accident. To forget the wonder, the terror, the utter finality of this fact, even for a moment, is to experience it again as if for the first time—one of the perils of traveling which we would learn over and over again.

But after long weeks of solitude, we finally needed to break out, to become part of life again, to be far away from everyone and everything in order to be closer to what, in any case, we are going through.

We have survived by cutting our life to the bone. The most ordinary gestures have become the most nourishing; the gaps between thoughts and memories the most necessary. But now, on the road, everything is on the clock. The outside has taken over from the inside, and we don't have enough spiritual muscle to resist. We bounce back and forth from paralysis to gathering information to compulsive distraction. Too many thoughts. Too many plans, or, as the Buddhists might say, too many attachments to the three poisons of addiction, aversion, and delusion.

Ironic. Before landing, Lynn had been saying what a relief it was not to be on some kind of demented "film trip," much more appropriate to be on a pilgrimage where we will allow all the levels of grief to unfold about Ayrev's death, a loss whose presence is inside us everywhere. But once again, a film net has dropped over me, as it has so often over the past twenty-five years. Part of me welcomes the intrusion. We are more exhausted and vulnerable than we could have imagined, and it will be a relief to let others navigate for us.

On the other hand, I feel compelled to push toward the margins of my "aloneness," to give in to alienation, exhaustion, and grief, not to mention the odd unexpected moment of wonder—because grief, as I have been learning, along with everything else it brings, can sometimes shatter ordinary self-absorption and vanity with such force that, for a moment, it seems to set one free. Until, that is, the tonic of self-congratulation sets in and one is reduced once again to the old encrusted and habitual patterns of personality.

The Buddha has a different take on the strategies of solitude. Talking to the old monk Thera, in the *Theranana Sutta*, he says:

> I will tell you how to achieve complete solitude. In the solitude that I am talking about, Thera, all that which is past must be relinquished. All which is in the future must be relinquished. Desire and lust in the present must be fully mastered. This is the way, Thera, that the true ideal of solitude can be completely realized. . . . The sage who overcomes everything, who knows everything, who is attached to nothing, who is completely free because he has renounced everything, who is with-

out thirst—he is the true sage. This man I call "one who lives alone."

But I do not "live alone," nor am I "without thirst." I am attached to Ayrev and to my memories of him and what his presence in my life meant to me, as the son I never thought I would have. And I am attached to my wife, to the rhythms of a life we have shared together for the past ten years. I am attached to the willful isolation of writing novels as much as to the raw, deluded "business" of making films. I am attached to escape, to the illusions of "the road" as well as to the barest "no exit" cul-de-sac. I am attached to studying Dharma and forgetting Dharma. And above all I am attached to my suffering, which is so inextricably wound up with pleasure and compensation.

Thus, it can be said, I am only a tourist on that broad avenue Lord Buddha referred to as the "middle way."

* * *

Neither alone nor together, neither in the present nor the past, we let Chatri, as he prefers to be called, guide us through customs.

Chatri is Thailand's foremost film director, with more than forty films and several Thai "Academy Awards" to his credit. A delicate middle-aged man with a trim mustache, wearing faded jeans, untucked white shirt, and untied Adidas, he seems, at first, to possess all the distracted casualness of an aristocratic world-class hippie, and yet one soon becomes aware of his insatiable curiosity and energy as he maneuvers, with an almost ferocious focus, through the eccentric complexities of life in a city that seems on the verge of gridlock and breakdown.

Outside the terminal, we step into the hot, humid night. There is no sense of the East, only the busy stench of the West.

Dharma quotes swim up. I can't stop them. They are beacons against my own subjectivity, which threatens, at times, to overwhelm me.

In the sky there is no East or West. We make these distinctions in the mind, then believe them to be true.

Everything in the world comes from the mind, like objects appearing from the sleeve of a magician.

—*Lankavatara Sutra*

We settle into Chatri's van, which not only transports him everywhere but also serves as his office, dining room, screening and family room. Immediately we are wrapped in the greasy envelope of Bangkok. Welcome to the future, to the worldwide culture of Nikes, Big

Macs, and bumper-to-bumper traffic endlessly creating paralysis, continual noise, and clouds of black car exhaust. The average speed of traffic in Bangkok is less than five miles per hour, and more than 70 percent of Thailand's energy consumption is used for transportation. Everywhere the chaos of overpopulation, ugly high-rises, video stores, advertising. Everyone plugged into business-as-usual by cordless phones, faxes, videos. Consumerism run amok.

After an endless drive we finally arrive at the Erawan Hyatt, a modern hotel in the middle of the city catering mostly to efficient Pacific Rim businessmen and stunned Western tourists.

In our room, which is a comfortably muted gray and beige, with the furniture possessing no cultural identity at all, we sleep fitfully, holding on to each other in our wretched dreams.

Waking in the middle of the night, I don't know where I am.

Suddenly, a stake through the heart. Where is Ayrev? Is he in the great ether, or has he already taken on another form? And who am I, anyway, and where am I going?

I remember the first line from one of Ayrev's last poems:

> I've fallen in love with the slowness of time,
> stillness and perceptions dancing.

Outside, there is still a hum of traffic, like a distant murmur of surf. Careful not to wake Lynn, I throw on jeans and a T-shirt and descend to the lobby. I walk around the block, remembering the phone call in the middle of the night that told us Ayrev had been killed in a car accident. He was driving all night to visit his father in Prescott, Arizona. He fell asleep . . . the car went off the road. . . .

When I return from my walk, it is five A.M. Lynn is in bed, looking up at the ceiling with tears, a strange half smile on her lips.

Where is my breathing? Where does it begin? Where does it end?

"Do not seek the truth," said Shankara the Monk. "Only cease to cherish opinions."

Dharma quotes continue to flap up against my psyche like old Band-Aids. They won't help. What would help would be to watch the display of mind rather than continually add to its compulsive business.

> When a thought arises, we must simply note that it has occurred, while at the same time remembering that it has come from nowhere, dwells nowhere and goes no-

where, leaving no trace of its passage, just as a bird, in its course across the sky, leaves no mark of its flight. In this way, when thoughts arise, we can liberate them into the absolute expanse. When thoughts do not arise, we should rest in the open simplicity of the natural state.

— DILGO KHYENTSE RINPOCHE

How desperate we are to liberate the one image that refuses to go away and dissolve it into the absolute expanse: Ayrev's body lying on the hospital gurney in Phoenix, beyond stillness, beyond silence, beyond hope.

* * *

After breakfast, we walk down Ploenchit Road for a few blocks in the thick gray smog, past the Hindu shrine on the corner where pilgrims make wishes, no doubt for an air-conditioned car or a condo way above it all. Bangkok feels like a scene from *Blade Runner*, a nightmare vision of the future—no air, no space. But everything and everyone busy. Buying, spending, scheming, and hustling. Drenched with sweat and fear, we retreat to the hotel.

In the *Nation*, Bangkok's morning newspaper, a first glimpse of modern Thai Buddhism:

An ex-monk, caught having sex with a female corpse in a coffin at a Samut Prakan Temple in January, was jailed for two years and six months and fined a total of Bt [baht] 1,000 on Friday by the provincial court.

However, judges Boonsong Noisopon and Lachit Chai-anong commuted the jail term by half after Samai Parnthong, 38, defrocked after the incident, pleaded guilty to the charge.

Samai, who was accused of other offences, was sentenced to eight months [in] jail for possessing 32.58 grammes of marijuana, two years for damaging other people's property, fined Bt 500 for engaging in a shameful act in public and fined Bt 5000 for creating a public nuisance after getting drunk.

But the ex-monk could not pay the fine and the court ordered that he serve an additional jail term instead at the rate of one day per Bt 12, the standard rate for all offenders.

In the afternoon we venture to the Oriental Hotel for tea with Chatri and Kamla, his attractive half-Indian, half-Thai wife who is also his producer, and their eight-year-old daughter, "Spider." The Oriental Hotel, along with the Raffles in Singapore, is, according to all the travel brochures, one of the last of the great nineteenth-century colonial hotels. What was once a refuge for such literary luminaries as Joseph Conrad, James Michener, Somerset Maugham, Paul Bowles, Graham Greene, and even Gore Vidal is now a haven for rich Americans and Europeans. It has been remodeled and brought up to date so that now it's just one more elegant international hotel. Oliver Stone, Brian DePalma, Roger Spottiswoode, and other Hollywood directors shooting Thailand for Vietnam drop anchor here along with Las Vegas and Monaco regulars on their way to Bali or the islands off the southern coast of Thailand. It's a stopover that manages to exclude everything "Oriental." The veranda by the pool and the well-appointed shops in the lobby selling Western and Eastern artifacts at outlandish prices could just as easily be in Beverly Hills or Palm Beach. Except, perhaps, for the great slimy Chao Phraya River flowing by like a sluggish grease trap.

After tea, we jump into a long, dugout-shaped tourist boat powered by an outboard motor. Skimming down the river, past kites wriggling like sperm against the gray background of factories and warehouses, we stop beside a boat train, a long chain of a dozen barges linked together that make the eight-day journey north to Chiang Mai and back again hauling sand and gravel. Chatri takes us on one of the barges, the stern of which is shaded by a tin roof. He has filmed these boat people before, and some of them remember him. An old white-bearded man, his frail body wrapped in a sarong, regards us with quiet dignity. A slender dugout slides alongside up and we buy tea and cookies from the river merchant.

We sit on the polished floorboards near the giant wooden rudder, for a brief moment witnessing a way of life that has existed for thousands of years. Whole families joined together with a common purpose, a floating community where everyone knows his role. No electricity. No television. No modern conveniences, not even plumbing. Only a simple Buddhist shrine next to a photograph of the king. All the food bought from floating grocery markets. A life of constant movement and change, seemingly removed from modern alienation and the ordinary horrors of dysfunctional family life — although who knows what really goes on. Perhaps the kids are desperate to leave such a simple life, whose values and interests are so similar. Perhaps some of them drift off into the urban ghetto, into adventure, drugs and rock 'n' roll, or, who knows, to a monastery to cultivate purity of conduct, unselfishness, and wisdom.

After the river jaunt, we stroll down Khao San, the hippie street made famous by the Indian-Vietnamese outlaw Sobhraj, who killed over fourteen tourists, many of them in this quarter, after hustling them with sex, charm, and phony business deals.

Rooms for five dollars a night. Shops selling tie-dyes, blue jeans, T-shirts, and cheap jewelry. It could be New York's Lower East Side or San Francisco's Haight Ashbury. The street is a sixties time warp, strangely senti-

11

mental and nostalgic. And yet there is little spontaneity among the foreign "hippies" and backpackers who stroll about in their Dead Head T-shirts and ponytails. It reminds me of Freak Street in Kathmandu, although cleaner and less funky.

Then back to the hotel and the little forest of arranged trees and bamboo in the lobby, which always seems to be occupied by squads of Japanese businessmen talking over their portable phones.

In the room, sudden grief and disorientation. Is it jet lag or my all-around exhaustion which causes a dive into such morose subjectivity? Or the poignancy of missing Ayrev, who would have prowled these streets with such vitality and enthusiasm? Both of them, no doubt, plus the overwhelming certainty that we should be anywhere but in Bangkok in the hottest time of the year. But as the sutras say, I am everywhere and nowhere: "What is born will die, what has been gathered will be dispersed, what has been accumulated will be exhausted, and what has been high will be brought low."

Our mood is just as suddenly challenged by an old rerun of Mary Tyler Moore on the English-language channel. We order club sandwiches from room service, sitting on the bed in our underwear, content to be comforted by the skillful rituals and canned laughter of an

American sitcom and by our cozy, insular isolation, which seems, for the moment, to be exactly the right combination to ease us into the night.

*   *   *

In the morning newspaper:

Once hidden from public view, alleged misconduct by Buddhist monks has increasingly made the headlines the past several years to tarnish the image of the revered Sangha institution. This ranges from minor charges of fortunetelling or giving tips on lottery numbers to serious charges of making personal gains from temple property or having sex with female worshippers.

The latest controversy involves Phra Thep Silvisut, the abbot of Wat Arun Ratchawararam. The abbot recently allowed a political rightist group to make use of the temple facilities and made a public statement praising military strongman Gen. Suchinda Kraprayoon, as the "right person" to become Thailand's prime minister.

In the eyes of several monks considered to be intellectuals among monks, the cause of the Sangha's decline is that it has stood still while other parts of the society have been changing rapidly.

For modern Thais, the Buddha's teachings might sound absurd to people in modern society. But that is social "karma" which reflects the ultimate truth of the Buddha's teaching on the natural law of cause and effect:

> As the seed, so the fruit:
> Do good, get good,
> Do bad, get bad.

Setting sight on the status of becoming a newly industrialized country, Thai society has adopted social values from the West. As a result, Thai people think that the desirable kind of progress is material progress.

It has become a national passion to reach for that economic miracle. In so doing, it has created a cultural distortion which focuses on an ever-increasing rate of consumption. The whole Thai way of life is altered, leading to rejection of religion and a decline in morality. The Sangha institution, now neglected, finds itself cut off from all movements of the outside world.

Chatri and Kamla take us on a tour of Patpong, Bangkok's world-famous sex quarter, comprising three streets in the middle of the banking and business quarter. A blazing display of neon signs, sex shops, and nightclubs where every imaginable sexual variation is for sale. The entire street is devoted to hustling desire. Full relief for your dollars from such clubs as The Playmate, The Pink Panther, the Lucky Strike Disco . . . sex, drugs, and rock 'n' roll. Every erogenous zone available for exploring, probing, penetrating. Even in this age of AIDS, the streets are jammed with American, European, and Japanese businessmen. The whole scene is so consumer-oriented and busy that one feels curiously removed, as if grazing through a huge super-market.

The first club we enter is a new four-story Las Vegas–style building hosting over a hundred girls, most of them sitting on tiers behind a large one-hundred-foot high plate-glass window. The girls are very young and beautiful in their elegant, high-necked silk evening gowns. As they chat among themselves, they seem totally oblivious of the array of men staring at them through the window. The whole display is like being in an exotic zoo.

Sex and death, pleasure and suffering . . . interesting and profound dichotomies to explore, but the bored mechanical sell of hard-core stimuli and crude fantasy ensure the absence of true relief. And as much as we might long to find release in sex and erotic rhythms, we have been through such a far greater intimacy with each other lately that the act of ingress itself seems somehow almost ludicrous.

> A man who does not pay attention where he walks will get bitten by a snake. Likewise sensual desires constitute serious dangers for the present and the future.
>
> —*Alagadadupama Sutta*

Monks, learn to keep watch at the doors of your senses. When you see material shapes, do not get immersed in the general appearance; do not get immersed in the details. If someone lives without controlling his sight, evil thoughts, greed, discouragement . . . find their way into him. So practice control of your sense of sight; keep watch on it; you must have complete control of the sense of sight. . . .

—Ganaka Moggallana Sutta

Thailand has over a quarter of a million monks and twice as many prostitutes. Chatri is researching a film about a young prostitute from northern Thailand whose father sold her to a brothel when she was fourteen, apparently a common transaction among the poverty-stricken hill tribes. Most girls send money home, and more than three-quarters of them, according to Chatri, will be dead of AIDS in three or four years. And yet this commerce goes on.

We check out one of the rooms: a round bed with a round mirror overhead, a bidet in the corner—everything neat and arranged.

We have Cokes in a darkly lit coffee shop while one of the girls demonstrates for us how she slips on a condom without the customer knowing it's on. Taking the condom out of her purse in one fluid motion, she blows it up and places it smoothly over a salt shaker. She smiles sadly.

Sometimes a customer refuses to wear the condom, and then she either jerks him off or gives him a blow job. She is eighteen, bored and very professional. She has no regrets. It's a living. "Karma," Chatri explains matter-of-factly. "Nothing one can do." And yet, like many Thais, he exists easily within many cultural contradictions, publicizing AIDS with his film and in newspaper interviews, spending time in hospitals with AIDS patients, and even carrying condoms on his key chain complete with instructions and information about this epidemic, which has already claimed millions of lives in his country.

Girls and their clients eat in the brothel's coffee shop, as well as, on this particular night, a table full of Japanese businessmen, two intensely animated drug dealers, a Polish tour group watching CNN on the huge TV, an abandoned drag queen, and a neighborhood family celebrating their daughter's birthday.

We visit a few other clubs. The most beautiful girls I have ever seen are dancing in white French lace bras and bikini underwear on top of a circular bar, their movements bored and solipsistic as they gently sway their hips to Diana Ross and the Supremes. They wear plastic tags around their necks with large numbers so that they can be easily identified. They also wear pendants on silver and gold chains engraved with images of the Buddha, which they only take off when they are servicing a customer.

Another club offers a live sex show performed by a bored young couple assuming three or four sexual positions in rapid succession. Afterward, the girl smokes a cigarette between the lips of her vagina. In another act, her partner, a handsome boy dressed in black leather, cracks a whip over her ass. They are a married couple. The man is a high school teacher during the day, a sex performer at night. He makes more in one week at the club than a year teaching school. But the burnout is extreme. He has to "get it up" eight times a day and doesn't know how long he can keep doing it.

In a dark, low-ceilinged bar packed wall to wall with customers, Chatri speaks to the owner, a plump man in a white suit smoking a huge cigar. The owner motions to one of the girls, who climbs on top of the bar, takes off her bikini briefs, and sticks a large crayon up her vagina. Placing a piece of white paper underneath her, she moves her pelvis around, writing "I love you Rudy" in big red letters. Then she hands me the paper. When I offer her some money, she refuses. "It is a gift."

The last bar we visit is gay. Pretty young boys, their eyes drugged and listless, dance together surrounded by middle-aged Western men. Many of the boys have

AIDS. The fat German sitting next to me slowly strokes the thigh of a boy who can't be more than fifteen. The German tells him how much he loves him, how much he turns him on. "Five hundred baht," the boy says—fifty dollars. "Then I love you, too."

We walk away from Patpong—a manifestation of hell, where death is a potential partner in any transaction and life seems less than impermanent. Ian Baruma, an English writer, makes this observation in his book *Gods and Dust*, part of the collection of travel and Dharma books I lug around with me:

> There appears to be an almost insulting contradiction between the image of the delicate Land of Smiles, of exquisite manners and "unique hospitality," and the world of live pussy shows. Yet, to see these images as contradictory is perhaps to misunderstand Thailand.
>
> Patpong kitsch and Thai traditions co-exist—they are images from different worlds, forms manipulated according to opportunity. The same girl who dances to rock 'n' roll on a bar top, wearing nothing but cowboy boots, seemingly a vision of corrupted innocence, will donate part of her earnings to a Buddhist monk the next morning, to earn religious merit. The essence of her culture, her moral universe outside the bar, is symbolized not by the cowboy boots, but by the amulets she wears around her neck, with images of Thai kings, revered monks, or of the Lord Buddha. The apparent ease with which Thais appear able to adopt different forms,

to swim in and out of seemingly contradictory worlds, is not proof of a lack of cultural identity, nor is the kitsch of Patpong proof of Thai corruption—on the contrary, it reflects the corrupted taste of Westerners, for whom it is specifically designed. Under the evanescent surface, Thais remain in control of themselves.

I wonder, having only known a few people who I ever felt were even remotely in control (including myself). In any case, my first impression of Thailand is of a country sliding out of control, an increasingly familiar situation around the world: societies full of violent attachments; dark, ungovernable fears; prowling hordes of *preta*s, or hungry ghosts; compulsively expanding, omnivorous populations governed by increasingly insatiable hates and addictions.

If there is any control, it is cold, not warm-blooded, and comes from that airless cubicle behind the "back room," the machine behind the machine that issues slick communication packages initiated by giant world corporations, promoting consumer progress, speed, and efficiency.

The Buddha said:

Manichulaka, I told those who needed grass to look for grass, those who needed wood to look for wood, those who needed transportation to look for transportation, those who needed an assistant to look for an assistant;

but I always told them not to seek nor to accept money
under any circumstances.

—Mahavagga

In Bangkok, capitalism has not just arrived but has
taken over. One feels the presence of huge corporations,
of decisions being made way beyond individual dis-
course, monocultural and global, coded from computers
and marketing polls. The beast has not only slouched
down the road, it has stayed for a huge meal. To be
present at such a feeding creates numbing aversion and
panic, as if the whole idea of self is somehow being
threatened with extinction.

But, as Dogen says: "What the Buddha means by the
Self is precisely the entire universe. Thus whether one
is aware of it or not, there is no universe that is not this
self. . . ."

The usual Buddhist catchphrase that material sur-
roundings are an illusion and only the internal world is
real doesn't reach me, because something else seems to
be at work here, a hallucinatory vision that questions
the very existence of the world itself, beyond internal
and external. Or is that just a failure of spiritual imagination, a dysfunctional inability to go with the "truth of
impermanence," with the "here-now-this" rather than
the "there-then-that"?

The Buddha taught that human existence is transient

and insubstantial, that attachment and aversion are the causes of suffering, and that learning nonattachment is the path to human happiness and freedom. Perhaps the environmental situation has gotten so extreme that a certain kind of attachment and aversion are necessary: attachment to the preservation of the world, aversion toward its destroyers, and a certain disregard toward personal freedom and happiness.

* * *

Lynn stays in the room while Chatri takes me to a birthday party for Princess Sirinhorn in the palace. By most accounts, the princess, King Bhumiphol's second daughter, is arguably the second most popular person in Thailand after her father. Both spend an enormous amount of time helicoptering around the kingdom initiating irrigation projects, hydroelectric plants, new dams, health centers, and so on, as well as reconstructing some of the more than twenty-seven thousand temples. Their reputations seem impeccable, although to a casual observer their efforts seem futile.

The princess is a large-boned, rather plain woman in her mid-thirties who greets everyone with the same quiet dignity, portraying a calm inner strength with a precise and wide-ranging intellect. Educated in the

West, she is fluent in five languages and is constantly involved in various projects, from the environment to AIDS.

The party is in a large hall full of her staff and relatives as well as various official dignitaries. Everyone greets her on their knees, offering beautifully wrapped presents as she works her way around the room. When she greets me, I want to ask her about Aung San Suu Kyi, the Burmese dissident and Nobel Prize winner now living under house arrest in Rangoon, who, I have heard, is a friend of hers, but before I can manage more than a *wai* (nod), she has passed me in the line to talk to an elderly woman about a hospice.

The whole feeling of "royal rituals" seems totally deadening and anachronistic, particularly when just a year ago, half a million Thais had rioted at Sanam Luong, demanding their right for constitutional rule. The richest army in the world had opened fire, killing thousands and causing martial law to be declared in Bangkok.

* * *

Back at the hotel, Lynn has been thinking about the current state of women in the Buddhist world. It seems that Thai society supports men who pursue lives of reli-

23

gious contemplation. Monks receive shelter and alms, but no such dispensations are made for women, who are almost totally excluded. Nuns are thought of as temple hands or, worse, as beggars. She shows me an article in the *Bangkok Post* about the Suan Wanasanti nunnery, where, three hours from Bangkok, a community of eighteen nuns *(bhikkuni)* have gathered together to form a religious community, growing their own food, part of which they sell for their common maintenance fund. The seventy-two-year-old mother superior, Khun Mae Yai, literally "Big Mother," has turned her inherited land into a self-sufficient community to help women with no financial means pursue religious lives. In the article, she comments on the present state of nuns:

> Women's lives are wasted because they are slaves to their husbands and children. They have no time for themselves to develop their spiritual potential. Women pursuing religious lives do not receive the same kind of social support as men. Women must have their own financial means in order to live as nuns, because the public does not make merit with us.
>
> I've seen many women crying, not wanting to leave the sisterhood but having to do so because their families cut their support. No one looks after nuns, so we have to look after ourselves.

The meditation technique used at Suan Wanasanti is to contemplate the disintegration of one's body until one sees the futility of clinging and realizes that one's duty is to be useful to others.

"The Bhikkuni effort still reflects an attachment to dogma and pride," Khun Mae Yai goes on. "All are actually equal in observing the precepts and cultivate spiritual strength. We are differentiated by karma, not by gender or status."

As she sees it, faith and respect cannot be commanded or come automatically with a formal *bhikkuni* order.

> You have to earn it through strict discipline, and for Bhikkuni it is much stricter than that of monks. And I doubt very much how many women in this time and age with lots of temptations and desires can properly fulfill their roles.
>
> As it is, fewer women want to be nuns than before. We used to have nearly forty people here. Now we only have eighteen.
>
> Besides, being Bhikkuni means being bound by so many rules that you end up being able to do nothing. It means living under the monks' order. It means being bound by ceremonial procedures.
>
> Why trade our independence for that?

No news from the English-Italian producer. It seems he has deserted us—as we, in our own way, have deserted him. We are still stuck in Bangkok, waiting for Chatri's van to be available to drive us to Sukhothai. We are helpless and frustrated, feeling the need to move, to flee this overload of information. It is as if we are stuck in a huge waiting room, our shoes nailed to the floor.

That night I see the princess again, at the annual film awards, Thailand's version of the Oscars. We spend an hour hanging out in the lobby of the auditorium, waiting for the princess to arrive, a passage which proves to be the best part of the show, certainly the most reverent, as literally everyone seems to love the princess. Finally she appears with her entourage, and everyone falls to their knees as she sweeps up the steps.

Chatri is not up for an award this year, and we sit through the ceremonies with no one to root for. The princess sits in front of the audience, facing the stage as the awards are presented by a blandly formal master of ceremonies who reads his script, followed by the winner kneeling on the floor to receive an award from the princess. Afterward there are songs and dances performed on the stage. The whole evening feels like a high school graduation, very safe and correct, possibly because of the presence of the princess, who normally isn't present at such functions.

All through the ceremonies I think of Bertolucci's film *Little Buddha* and those parts of the script I wrote for him, a process which took almost a year and which ended with a bad case of burnout and self-recrimination. How huge and oversized the budget was compared to Thai films, or, for that matter, most Third World films, all of which seem to be made on budgets of under five hundred thousand, fifty times less than the average Hollywood film. Not that the Thais are consciously adopting a philosophy of "Less is more" or concentrating on substance rather than manipulative effect. If they could, they, like everyone else, would make films with absolutely no content or artistic intentions for as much money as possible. Writing the Bertolucci script, I felt bound to the dichotomies of hope and fear. Sacred and profane. Success and failure. Even though I've been a student of the Dharma off and on for over twenty-five years, in India and Nepal as well as in the States, I knew just enough about Buddhism to realize that I knew very little at all, particularly when it came to writing about it for a mass audience.

One evening in New York, when I was in the early stages of the script, I took Bertolucci to meet a Tibetan lama, Gelek Rinpoche, in an effort to satisfy a list of questions we had struggled with about the meaning of reincarnation and karma. Before answering our questions, Gelek Rinpoche, who has lived in the United States for over ten years and who speaks very fluent English, looked at me and said abruptly, "The first thing you should do is take off your Buddhist clothes." I was never really successful. My Buddhist clothes remained tightly wrapped around me, almost to the point of choking me. I could never let go of my self-consciousness. I was too determined to please and too afraid of failure to follow the advice of my teacher, His Holiness Dudjom Rinpoche, who said in one of his writings: "Let go in the free natural flow of uncontrived awareness." I wasn't enough of a Buddhist to drop being a Buddhist. The whole view of the film seemed too pious, too politically correct. I probably would have been more useful if I had been more innocent, even more ignorant—certainly less uptight and not so awkwardly and continually pondering Buddhist views, such as the third-century Buddhist philosopher Nagarjuna's statement that the things of the phenomenal world possess no phenomenal essence. I was too aware that even a film on the life of the Buddha can become another quick fix, another reductive distraction for a passive audience, another hors d'oeuvre for hungry ghosts, and, of course, ultimately, nothing more substantial than yesterday's newspaper-magazine-film-TV entertainment.

*   *   *

Back in our room, my mind is still cruising through reflections of the past.

At first, in the late sixties and early seventies, writing scripts was a welcome relief from the internal and, in those days, solipsistic journey of living inside one of my novels. Writing an occasional script seemed to offer a livelihood that would keep me away from teaching fiction, a fate I was determined to avoid at any cost, as I have yet, to this day, to discover what fiction is. Nor do I want to. I prefer to keep the jeopardy of that process to myself. And such was my convoluted and obsessive relationship to language that I welcomed, as a relief and antidote, the first axiom of the screenwriter, which is to sublimate language to image. The other, more personal sublimations would come later and cause far greater damage, such as strip-mining the imagination and cherishing and exploiting the illusions of nonexistent self, the opposite of doing what the great nineteenth-century Dzogchen master Patrul Rinpoche suggests, cutting "the rope of hope and expectation, since it cannot benefit anyone."

If you lose your own peaceful center and are overwhelmed by the force of others and by intellectual perceptions and emotional feelings generated by external circumstances, then your own mind will have no independence, freedom, or peace and you will be functioning in terms of others as a slave.

—TULKU THUNDOP

> The Victorious One [the Buddha] said: "All phenomena are like magic." But what greater magic is there than the present age? Enticing magicians are performing; fear the beguiling, hypnotizing phantoms of the Kali Yuga [the Sanskrit name for the degenerate age we live in, known as the "end of the end"].

We visit the Asia Bookstore. At the end of a shelf are a few books on and by Thomas Merton, the Trappist monk from the Abbey of Gethsemani. I scan a book of memoirs about him, looking for information about his death in a Bangkok hotel room in 1968 where he was accidentally electrocuted by a fan. Moved by his death, and by his openness to Buddhism, I write down a quote from Thich Nhat Hanh, who considered himself a close friend of Merton's:

> Merton had a good understanding of Buddhism. One of the most difficult things concerning the understanding between the East and West is that the West tends to think in a dualistic way. But in the East, if Buddha exists, then Mara (the god of desire and death) should exist also. Merton could see that the two are two faces of the same reality. And that we must not create a battle between them; we should have peace and reconciliation without making any effort. . . .
>
> I don't make any distinction between being and doing. Sometimes we do very much, but not for the sake of peace. Sometimes we do not do anything, but we are for peace. So instead of saying, "Don't just sit there,

do something," we can say the opposite: "Don't just do something, sit there."

And this from Merton's journal, written six months before his Asian journey:

> I realize that I have a past to break with—an accumulation of inertia, waste, wrong, foolishness, rot, junk. A great need of clarification, of mindfulness, or rather, of no-mind. A return to genuine practice, right effort. Need to push on the great doubt. Need for the spirit. Hang on to the clear light.

Would the East finally have given him what he was searching for? Would the "great doubt" have opened him further, pushing him beyond his own descriptions, to confront the emptiness within all of his compulsive form?

And what have my own journeys to the East over the past twenty-five years given me, other than exotic adventure and temporary relief from American culture? Spiritual vertigo, certainly, followed by a long, gradual pull toward an internal, if often awkward definition of life that didn't include failure and success, fame or materialism. These journeys were often accompanied by moments of hilarious inattention, as when I flew back to Los Angeles after a retreat in Nepal to meet with the head of a studio about directing a western that I had written. Sitting in the huge, overstuffed leather couch in his office, I was literally unable to speak or even remember exactly what I was there for. The project was dismissed out of hand, and the next day I flew back to Kathmandu, only to be so disoriented that I stayed inside my hotel room for ten days. Compare this to the total ease of Tibetan lamas who fly from the inaccessible mountains of northern Nepal or even feudal Tibet directly to New York, cruising through phenomena with such lucid ease that they never miss a beat and begin teaching Dharma the next day, neither coming nor going.

* * *

But we have arrived and are waiting to go, although knowing what day it is or what exactly we should be doing has largely disappeared. We are punchy and impatient and already burned out with too much information. Our room increasingly reflects our minds: half-empty trays, stacks of cookies, old newspapers and discarded travel books. Once, Dudjom Rinpoche described mindfulness to a roomful of Westerners as that state you are in when you wake up in the morning in a strange motel in a strange city and for a moment you don't know where you are; your mind is empty of information and chitchat, and you just sit there, alert and at ease and full of wonder. "Whatever perceptions arise," he said, "you should be like a little child going into a beautifully decorated temple; he looks, but grasping does not enter into his perception at all. . . ." In this state, perception "falls apart with the abandon of a madman."

Which is not the state of our minds when we lunch with Sterling Siliphant, Michael Wadleigh, Chris Moore, Chatri, and Kamla in the lavish hotel restaurant, which offers a buffet of Thai and Western food. The local "ex-pats," myself included, fall easily into cynical film gossip and grandiose, deluded schemes. Sterling Siliphant, the former Hollywood screenwriter, probably best known for *In the Heat of the Night*, which garnered him an Oscar, is a robust figure in his seventies who seven or eight years ago split Hollywood for good. He couldn't take "all the bullshit"; also he loves Bangkok, particularly the women, of which he seems to have several, "the younger the better." Michael Wadleigh, the director of *Woodstock*, among other films, and an old "Eastern hand" who has traveled widely throughout Southeast Asia and who now is obsessed with making a documentary about Aung San Suu Kyi, and Chris

Moore, an American writer living in Bangkok who has written several novels about expatriates living in Thailand.

It is relaxing and at the same time disturbing, this feed with the ex-pats. We share lots of common ground about the horrors of L.A. and the film business, conceiving a mad, idealistic plan about making three or four films back to back with everyone sharing in the whole package. If Chatri can do one for four hundred thousand, why can't we do three for five million? We'll start a film commune. Chatri will direct one, I will direct or write one on spiritual art theft, possibly from André Malraux's first novel, set in Cambodia, *The Royal Way*. Sterling will write an adaptation of Chris's book *The Killing Smile*, and Wadleigh will write about the student riots in Bangkok or Aung San Suu Kyi. We'll be forever free, independent, rich, and courageous—and so busy we won't have to know about the rest of anything, including ourselves.

In the middle of the meal, drunk and disoriented, I take a break, drifting into the men's room to wash my face, then holding my head in my hands as I sit down on the john. A book falls out of my jacket pocket: Joseph Goldstein's guide to Buddhist meditation, *The Experience of Insight*. I have been reading it as a simple guide to Theravadan practice, that form of Buddhism, known as the Hinayana, which is common throughout Southeast Asia. In front of me is an instruction about eating:

> Opening the mouth. Putting in the food. Closing the mouth. The intention to lower the arm, and then the movement. One thing at a time. Feeling the food in the mouth, the texture. Chewing. Experience the movement. As you begin chewing, there will be taste sensations arising. Be mindful of the tasting. As you keep on chewing, the taste disappears. Swallowing. Be aware of the whole sequence involved. There is no one behind it, no one who is eating. It's merely the sequence of intentions, movements, tastes, touch sensations. That's what we are—a sequence of happenings, of processes, and by being very mindful of the sequence, of the flow, we get free of the concept of self.

I return for dessert and more drinking with the expats, all of us, each in our own way, promoting and toasting the "concept of self." After lunch, Lynn goes to a camera store, and I collapse in our room and sleep for the rest of the day.

> If we lose ourselves in memories of situations involving desire, hatred, pride, and jealousy, then we chain ourselves more securely to delusion. It is through preoccupation with these kinds of situations that karma develops and suffering ensues.
>
> —Dilgo Kyentse Rinpoche

Or, as Virgil said: "Hell is easy to enter and very hard to get out of."

* * *

Waking up hung over in the middle of the night, with Lynn quietly crying next to me, I think of the pain of Kisha Gautami, who lost her son. As recounted in the sutras, she went from house to house, asking for medicine to bring her son back. But everyone laughed at her, until she brought her request to the Buddha. He listened to her request and then advised her:

"You did well, Kisha Gautami," he replied, "in coming here for medicine. Listen to me carefully. Go back to the city, begin at the beginning, and bring me a fistful of mustard seed from the first house in which no one has ever died."

"I will do so, holy one," she said gratefully.

Joyfully she entered the first house and said, "The holy one wants me to bring him a fistful of mustard seed as medicine for my son. Can you give me mustard seed?"

They brought out a mustard seed and gave it to her.

"Has anyone died in this house?" she asked.

"They have never stopped dying," they replied. "So many deaths . . ."

"Take back the seed," Kisha Gautami said. "The holy one told me not to bring mustard seed from a house in which a death has taken place."

"Poor Gautami," they said. "The dead are everywhere."

She went to a second house, to a third, and a fourth. There must be *one* without a death in it! The Buddha could not have been so cruel. He would have had some pity on her.

She could not find a single house to bring mustard seed from.

She took her son to the cremation ground, holding him before her in her arms.

"O my little son, my dear son," she said, "I thought that when you died, only you died. But death is everywhere. It is a universal law—all must die. Village law, market law, house law are passing; only this law is eternal." She placed her child on the cremation ground and went back to the Buddha.

"Kisha Gautami," he asked, "did you get the mustard seed?"

"Holy one," she replied, "enough of this business of the mustard seed! Only give me refuge."

*   *   *

We are invited for dinner at the home of Orin, an old Dharma bum from Australia who now lives off Sukumvit Road in Bangkok. I knew him in the seventies in Kathmandu, where he was hanging out on the fringes of the Tibetan scene. I would see him occasionally at the giant Tibetan stupa in Bodhnath or at teachings of celebrated lamas, or lounging on the temple steps of Pashupatinath, smoking bhang with the wild-haired Shaivite yogis on the banks of the Bagmati River. He also was an occasional poet and art smuggler who, after he was busted for opium on the Indian border, went into retreat for three years in a monastery north of Darjeeling. Now he's a respectable Oriental art dealer who journeys to London, New York, Paris, and Hong Kong, selling his wares, most of which are stolen Buddhist sculptures and paintings from all over Southeast Asia, Tibet, and Nepal.

Orin, who is now overweight and puffy, with huge bags underneath his bulbous, restless eyes, lives in a modern duplex apartment in a quiet cul-de-sac with his young Laotian wife, who never says a word during the entire dinner. As her husband's guests eat from an abundant South Indian cuisine that she has spent the entire day preparing, she bows and serves and smiles. Around us, outlined in a soft aura of candlelight, are

Tibetan rugs, Indian erotic paintings, and mostly Thai
and Cambodian sculptures of Buddhist deities. Several
other people are present: a former Tibetan Buddhist nun
from New Jersey, now a translator; a Thai film producer;
and a strung-out rug dealer from Kathmandu by way of
Santa Cruz. Most of the dinner conversation is gossip
about the comings and goings of various lamas, old
Western Dharma casualties, rumors about the new in-
carnation of the Karmapa (the spiritual authority of the
Karma Kagyu school of Tibetan Buddhism), tantric
teachings in Bodhgaya, and the collapse of Kathmandu
and Bangkok from the ravages of expansion, government corruption, and materialism. The present strategy
of survival for "old Eastern hands" is to put down stakes
in dreamy agrarian backwaters such as Laos and Vietnam, anywhere but the nightmare cities of India and
Southeast Asia.

After dinner, our host takes us upstairs to show us
his latest acquisitions: nine thirteenth-century wooden
statues that were discovered in, then stolen from, a cave
in northeastern Thailand. They are in almost perfect
condition, except for a figure of Manjushri, who is missing the arm that holds his sword of wisdom.

"I can probably move all nine at the Met," Orin says
proudly. I look at Lynn. We have become almost un-

bearably depressed. All the chat, the hip deals, the pillaging of artifacts, the compulsive cultural and spiritual mutations, make us want to flee.

Orin is suddenly defensive: "They'll go into a museum anyway. I'll just be a well-paid midwife."

We wish him the best of luck and take a taxi home, pleading fatigue.

* * *

The next day, we sleep and order room service and stare vacantly out the window at the stalled traffic. We have hit a slump. Neither of us feels like continuing, and we even contemplate flying back to our home in Hudson Valley or finding a place on the beach in southern Thailand for a few weeks. But we are nailed to fulfilling Lynn's photo assignment. Perhaps it is just as well; without obligations we would be no more than matchboxes on the ocean. Rather than being on a pilgrimage, even a failed one, we would be on a vacation or, worse, an adventure. And going back will be as arduous and melancholy as going forward, because most of the time we both know there isn't any difference.

In the evening, Chatri appears in the lobby with Wadleigh and takes us out to his family compound, where he is building a new house. Most of his family, including his two sisters and mother and father, live next to one another on a commonly owned plot of land. They are separate and yet together, a real antidote to the contemporary malaise and alienation of Bangkok. As if to reinforce this idea of relaxed community, he takes us to dinner at a simple restaurant on a quiet street that his mother- and father-in-law run with the help of their two sons. Everyone is included, just as Chatri's films include both relatives and friends, an extended family that manages, somehow, to work with one another.

Our last day in Bangkok, Lynn, Wadleigh, and I visit Sulak Sivaraksha, a leading Buddhist scholar, lawyer, and social activist, who was recently nominated for the 1994 Nobel Peace Prize by Mairead Corrigan, herself a winner of the prize from Northern Ireland. Under house arrest by the government, Sulak receives us at his home, two or three modest wooden buildings in the middle of a narrow street of tall high-rises. His is the only building that is not modern and over two stories tall.

Last week was his sixtieth birthday, and tomorrow he will face prosecution on charges of insulting the king and defaming former army chief general Suchinda Krapayoon. If found guilty, he could be jailed for seventeen years. But he seems totally relaxed as he offers us tea in his garden, his lawyer sitting quietly by his side. He wears a white collarless cotton shirt, loose cotton trousers with a *pha khamah* (loincloth) as a belt, and comfortable slippers. We talk about everything from Coca-Cola (he's against it as a form of cultural imperialism) to Bhutan (he thinks the rigidity and conservatism of its Buddhist king and government will inevitably cause it to fall).

Even though Siam (he rejects "Thailand," a name imposed by the West) was never colonized by a Western power, it has been totally conquered by Western consumerism. "Look at any street in Bangkok. All you see are people defining themselves by Western advertising. Today Bangkok is a third-rate Western city."

We can only agree. But then, of course, every city in the world is beginning to be a third-rate city. Wadleigh, whose lean, whippetlike features make him look like an aging greyhound, all sinew and sniffing nose, ready to run after any concept, any cause as long as it means action, asks Sulak for advice about a film he wants to do, a kind of East-West *Woodstock*, fusing Asian and Western rock bands. A "We're all one world" idea. Where does Sulak think they could hold it? In the park? Outside the city? In a stadium? Sulak is polite, but it's obvious we've lost him on this one.

Lynn brings the conversation back to consumerism, which causes him to brighten a bit. It's obviously one of his favorite subjects. Again, Wadleigh jumps in with a long riff about Adidas, Reeboks, TV, record companies, Aung San Suu Kyi, Steven Spielberg, and monocultural advertising jingles. Not missing a beat, Sulak plays the same chord: Department stores have become Siamese shrines. *Development* has become a euphemism for *greed*. After World War II and more intensely with the Vietnam War, America came into Siam and exploited the natural wealth as quickly and efficiently as possible. With consumer culture came sexual exploitation, violence, and drug abuse. Consumerism exploits the minds and bodies of the young. Modern Siam is an eroding society. In Bangkok we see traffic jams and pollution, but we cannot see human values. He goes on to say that importing Western ideas haphazardly without properly understanding one's native culture and the foreign culture from which the ideas come leads to a struggle between two forces: *wattanatham* (rural culture) and *wattanatham muang* (urban culture). "In a rural culture, everyone is equal. Buddhism is at the center of everyone's hearts, people respect and care for each other. But over the past thirty years, this very culture has been destroyed and mutilated because of an imported urban culture. A rural and traditional culture is essential; life lived for oneself is meaningless."

We chat about the relevancy of Gandhi to Buddhism,

about air travel, New York, and his trial, which he thinks will be postponed (which, in fact, it was), and then swing back to Buddhism and the three poisons: greed, hatred, and delusion. All three are manifestations of unhappiness, and the presence of any one poison breeds more of the same. Capitalism and consumerism are driven by these three poisons. As Sulak points out in a recent book, *Seeds of Peace:*

> Consumerism supports those who have economic and political power by rewarding their hatred, aggression and anger. And consumerism works hand in hand with the modern educational system to encourage cleverness without wisdom. It teaches people to look down on their own indigenous, self-reliant culture in the name of progress and modernization. We need to live simply in order to subvert the forces of consumerism and materialism. . . . Buddhists should go back to the teachings of Buddha on life and death for a peaceful and just society where individual moral and spiritual growth is nourished, and where the wholeness of life is affirmed.

This is not a simple idea, given the fact that consumerism is rampant worldwide and that Thai Buddhism is a state religion in which spiritual life is inevitably corrupted and compromised.

Sulak agrees. "Siam is the only country where a Buddhist monarchy remains, where Buddhism, the monar-

chy, and nationalism are inseparable. But if you chal-
lenge this reality, you could end up in jail, as I might
tomorrow. In any case, if Buddhism becomes too nation-
alistic, it will die, which is what happens with state reli-
gions."

Sulak gives us a few packages to mail for him in the
States, and we say goodbye. As I look back to wave, he
is already engaged in a heated conversation with his
lawyer, who is furiously taking notes.

* * *

The next morning, before sunrise, we leave for
Chiang Mai by way of Sukhothai, the thirteenth-century
capital of the first large Thai kingdom in Siam, as well
as a stop at Tham Krabok, a rehab monastery. Chatri
has provided a van for us with a driver as well as the
two guides who had also met us when we first arrived
at the airport; his brother-in-law, Gee; and Anna, his
girlfriend. Even though we leave before five A.M., it
takes several hours of driving through the usual con-
gested traffic to finally free ourselves of Bangkok.

It is a long, boring drive over a straight, well-paved
highway, past parched fields, an occasional rice paddy,
and modern gas stations and sandwich shops.

After four hours, we pull in to Tham Krabok, a temple complex visible from the road surrounded by craggy limestone hills. *Tham Krabok* means "Opium-Pipe Cave Monastic Center." Its main function is to serve as a detox haven for people with a wide variety of addictions, from opium and crack to alcohol and even cigarettes. It is famous for having cured tens of thousands of drug addicts from Thailand as well as many other countries, including the West and Australia. Lately the government has claimed that the abbot, Phra Chamroon Panchan, who was a policeman before he became a Buddhist monk, is allowing Tham Krabok to harbor illegal Lao immigrants who are trying to coordinate subversive activities against the communist government in Vientiane. Phra Chamroon denies all charges, saying that the thirteen thousand Hmong tribesmen in his community were all involved in the opium trade in the Golden Triangle and couldn't care less about overthrowing the Laotian or any other government.

I feel immediately at home in Tham Krabok, being somewhat of an aficianado of *tanhas*, or cravings. It is an excellent place to contemplate the five central facts of Buddhism:

1. I am subject to decay, and I cannot escape it.
2. I am subject to disease, and I cannot escape it.
3. I am subject to death, and I cannot escape it.
4. There will be separation from all that I love.

5. I am the owner of my deeds. Whatever deed I do, good or bad, I shall become heir to it.

The whole place is funky and hard-core. Walking down a dirt path toward the main temple, we pass a huge black iron Buddha sitting at the head of a rock quarry, surrounded by rusting machinery as well as twenty-five statues of his main disciples, all made from iron. Behind the quarry, a rocky mountain is surrounded by thick jungle.

Tham Krabok was founded by Mae-chii Mian, a Buddhist nun. Twenty-five percent of the three-hundred-person staff are nuns, the rest monks. All monks or nuns help with the program, and more than half have been addicts themselves.

We sit at a small stone table underneath the shade of a huge tree, watching the patients lounge around languidly in their red cotton pants behind a closed courtyard while others seem free to wander around the compound, smoking cigarettes and chatting among themselves. Most of them seem to be teenagers or in their twenties. A lot of them have intricate tattoos. Seventy percent, we learned later, are Asian, mostly from Thailand, Burma, and Cambodia, while the rest are Westerners. No women are visible; they must be in separate quarters.

The main part of the program involves an emetic

herbal treatment. For five days every morning the patient drinks a thick concoction of 150 different herbs, followed by a sauna in the afternoon, and then, in the evening, the patients gather for a group purge, kneeling in lines in front of a long cement trough and puking their guts out. The session is often accompanied by loud pulsating music played by other patients who have already gone through this part of the process. After five days of sweating and vomiting there follow another twenty-five days of meditation, herbal saunas, and counseling. Before being admitted, the potential patient takes a vow to abide strictly by the rules of the monastery. He writes the vow on a piece of rice paper and then swallows it. If he breaks even one rule, he is immediately thrown out and can never come back again. It's hardball, all or nothing, and for the most part, it seems to work, as Phra Chamroon claims over a seventy percent success rate.

A black American monk, Gordon—or Monk Gordon, as he prefers to be called—broke it down further for us. "I'll tell you one thing, dude, most of the people who go back on their vow seem to die. *Tanha* [grasping, or desire] is *tough,* baby. No prisoners. That's the way it is when you're dealing with *tanha* or *dukkha* [suffering]. We got all kinds coming here from all over the world. We group 'em according to their religion and sex. We change their name, give 'em vegetarian food, and put 'em through the process. We have one monk for every ten addicts. That's first-class treatment any way you cut it."

Monk Gordon is a broad-shouldered, middle-aged ex-junkie from Harlem who has fought as a mercenary in the Falkland Islands, South Africa, and Cambodia, as well as in Vietnam. As the only resident foreign senior monk among the monastery's clergy, he has made a vow to stay for life and has already been at Tham Krabok for over ten years.

His approach is straightforward. No bullshit, no "idiot compassion." He gets the job done. "We mostly get 'em eight to forty-five years old. The younger the better. Lot of these kids got strung out from their mama blowing opium up their nostrils, to chill them out. Lot of 'em coming down from the Golden Triangle. Not to mention the South Bronx.

"Each patient gets five visits and then only from a relative for not more than twenty minutes. We watch 'em. They blow this chance, most likely they blow it all."

Being a monk at Tham Krabok demands a lot of discipline. Aside from dealing with the addicts, there are other chores, such as breaking rock at the quarry, making your own robes, cutting wood, planting rice, growing the herbal plants (whose mixture is a secret), and building and repairing all the structures on the 350-acre grounds, not to mention finding time to meditate. When I ask Monk Gordon about *vipassana*, or insight meditation, he says they all do it but in different ways. The most common way of measuring how long to meditate is by how long it takes to burn an incense stick, or *cello*— around forty minutes. He himself is a "500-stick-a-year man."

The monks also eat only one meal a day and renounce all forms of transportation, except walking. Every year, just before the rainy-season retreat, the monks go on *thudong,* or forest walking, for a few weeks, taking only a parasol and mosquito net. They sleep on the forest floor and never stay in one place more than a night.

Abruptly, Monk Gordon stands up. "I don't say good-bye," he says. "I only say hello."

Turning away from us, he walks down the path.

*   *   *

The van drives past the same views of dry fields and modern gas stations, a Thai version of our own Midwest. Anna puts a video of one of Chatri's films on the VCR, *Salween,* an epic about life on the Salween River in Thailand's lawless border areas with Burma. The film involves the local police and the Karen, one of the Burmese hill tribes, as well as unscrupulous Thai logging tycoons. It is bloody and professionally made, but my mind is too distracted to focus on the violent images of slaughter and betrayal, and after a while I fall asleep.

Finally, after four hours, we stop at Lop Buri to visit a small cluster of temples in the middle of the city, influenced by sculpture brought into Thailand from Cambodia and built by Khmer artisans between the tenth and fourteenth centuries. Initially I had been interested in this site because of the visual transition between the Mahayana and Theravadan influences, but the temples seem heavy and undistinguished to my untrained eye. The grounds are full of monkeys scampering everywhere in an endless quest for garbage and treats offered by tourists. The monkeys are arrogant and fearless, and one climbs up on Lynn, pulling her hair. Another one steals two rolls of film from her pocket and runs off with it. Sitting high up on a terrace on one of the temples, it looks at us disdainfully as it unrolls the film, which includes all the shots of Monk Gordon and Tham Krabok.

The intense heat is getting to me as we continue down the long, still-tedious highway toward Sukhothai, the ancient center of Thai civilization. Stomach cramps, hot and cold sweats, headaches.

We finally arrive at the Sukhothai Hotel, a large, two-story cement pile with rooms set around a circular courtyard, a large swimming pool in the middle. Because this is the hot season, no one is about. The whole place feels sterile and oddly fascistic. It reminds me of the Japanese hotel at Lumbini Grove, near Siddhartha's birthplace of Kapilavastu in what is now southern Nepal: cold, charmless, antiseptic, constructed for large tour groups who just want to bop in to one of the major Buddhist holy spots, grab some "merit," snap a few photos, buy a souvenir or plastic relic to take home, and *sayonara*, on to Bodhgaya or Bodhnath or Borobudur, other stops on the pilgrimage circuit.

We collapse in our room. An hour later I'm too wiped out to take a look at the ruins, and Lynn leaves without me. I drink a glass of ice water. Almost immediately my stomach goes into convulsions. I actually think I'm going to pass out. Ripping off my clothes, I crawl into the bathroom and roll around on the tile floor. My breath comes in desperate gasps. I don't think of anything or anyone, just the pain. My mind is obscure and totally unclear. I have no detachment, no view that includes its opposite, no sense that I am not my body. I am a low, writhing mess of sensational pain and fear.

Another delicious reduction on "the road to nowhere." That morning I had been reading from Patrul

Rinpoche's little book, *The Practice of the Essence of the Heart Jewel, View, Meditation and Action* and had underlined two stanzas, thinking of Ayrev, who had died in a "blink," asleep at the wheel, at the pinnacle of his twenty-one-year-old energy cycle: magnetic, driven, passionate, strangely wise and poetic—and then he was gone, and here I am flopping around the bathroom floor of a grotesque tourist hotel in Sukhothai like an old frog.

For a moment I think I'm dying. I am totally alone, without help, without wisdom, without the dependable muscle of a real practice to guide me; no *bardo* prayers, no instructions, no spaciousness, no image of my root guru, or any teacher, for that matter, not even a friend, or my wife, or even my dog. All I am left with is fear and pain.

For some reason, as if it's going to help, I crawl over to my suitcase and look for Patrul Rinpoche's stanzas.

Hoping in others with false smiles,
the self pretends with expectation,
doing this and that with hopes and doubts.
Now, when this occurs, do nothing.
Even if death comes today, do not regret leaving
     samsaric Dharma.

Even if a hundred years are survived, still, passing
     youth is not joyful.

Whether death or life comes, so what?
To accomplish Dharma for the next life is enough.

Burn this old attachment corpse in the fire of
    nonattachment.
Practice essence Dharma with present phenomena, this
    contains seven periods.
Accumulated merit is a smoke offering,
perfectly dedicated to the deceased, so recite the six
    syllables.

I try to read the words again because my eyes won't focus. In fact, Patrul Rinpoche's authority and wisdom mind seem so far away from me that I put the book back in the suitcase and turn on the TV. The only station is CNN. Larry King is interviewing Julia Roberts.

Lynn finds me on the bathroom floor, wallowing and moaning on the cool tiles. Calmly, she makes me take three acidophilus pills and a Valium, and almost immediately the pain is gone.

Life is precious, unbearably precious.

I'm back to my old self, although too weak to eat. But tomorrow, for sure, I'll be out rummaging through the ruins of Sukhothai as if nothing had ever happened, having witnessed nothing and learned less.

That night, I'm sick again. This time, the attack is even worse. But the same treatment rescues me once more. I lie on the bathroom floor within easy access to the toilet and think about the Thai word *khwan*, which means "life spirit." Anyone, according to Thai folk custom, can lose their *khwan*. It happens when some great shock occurs to the psyche, such as a death or a betrayal of one's integrity, that puts a dent in your immune system or the center of your being. It defeats your spiritual protectors. In the West it's called depression or melancholia. A common enough complaint from middle-aged writers who have spent too much time on the celluloid trail, giving away their language to directors and producers, sublimating their "self" to the outside, betraying their own signature, becoming, in a sense, a slave to others.

Spiritually this condition probably originates from the endless breaking of vows, from not following through after receiving the gift of transmission into a certain practice. It comes from living a distracted life too far away from mindfulness.

How do I get my *khwan* back? By the "action of nonaction." By saying no with discriminating awareness. By abandoning superficial ambitions which are full of aggression and ego enhancements.

A prayer from Dudjom Rinpoche recalls the necessary view which sustains the *khwan:*

> May we obtain the Great Confidence of the view,
> Where both *samsara* and *nirvana* are one.*
>
> May we greatly perfect and strengthen meditation,
> Which is naturally resting in the unaltered state.
>
> May we greatly accomplish the action,
> Of nonaction, which is naturally accomplished.
>
> May we self-find the *dharmakaya*,†
> Which is free of obtaining and abandoning."

I think of Ayrev and how full of spirit he was before he died. I'm not angry, nor do I feel betrayed. I feel not so much empty as raw and unsettled. I'm shocked at the paucity of my Dharmic view, how subjective I am, how indulgent with my emotional pain. Frightened at how

---

Samsara: The "cycle of existences," a succession of rebirths that a being goes through within the various modes of existence until liberation is attained. Imprisonment in *samsara* is conditioned by the three "unwholesome roots": hatred, craving, and delusion.

Nirvana: The goal of spiritual practice in all branches of Buddhism. The term *nirvana* does not indicate annihilation, but rather entry into another mode of existence. Nirvana is unconditioned; its characteristic marks are absence of arising, subsisting, changing, and passing away.

†*Dharmakaya* ("body of the great order"): The true nature of the Buddha, which is identical with transcendental reality, the essence of the universe. The *dharmakaya* is the unity of the Buddha with everything existing. At the same time, it presents the Dharma, the teaching expounded by the Buddha.

much time I've wasted. In front of me now is the inevitable display of sickness, old age, and death—if, indeed, I'm fortunate enough to be able recognize the drama of the "last act" as it unfolds.

The next morning Lynn has already left when I take a taxi out to the ruins, passing the Yom River, which flows through the entire site, over fifty miles across a flat plain bordered by low mountains in the far distance. The city was once the center of a kingdom that included Luang Prabang on the Mekong River in Laos, lower Burma, and Malacca in Malaysia.

It is hot and still. Only a few orange-robed monks are walking slowly along the side of the empty street with their begging bowls—the opposite of what Sukhothai must have been like when it was the first Thai kingdom of Siam, reaching its zenith between 1257 to 1389 under the reign of King Ramkhamhaeng. This warrior king, in addition to extending the kingdom, unified art and architecture into an expression dominated by Buddhism, an ornate and elegant style that was greatly influenced by the art of Sri Lanka, and, to an extent, India. So abstract and stylized are most of the sculpted figures that the fingers and toes of Buddha often look the same.

The wats in Sukhothai are surrounded by pools, symbolizing the notion that the heavens are contained by the primordial ocean. Religious buildings face the water, out of remembrance of the Buddha, who sat under the Bodhi Tree facing a river when he attained enlightenment. When natural water wasn't available, the monks dug ponds.

At Wat Mahathat, I catch a glimpse of Lynn's head, her long, prematurely white hair bowed like a silver curtain over her camera as she stands before a statue of a standing Buddha over thirty feet tall. Around her are large broken columns and *chedis*, called stupas in India and Tibet, pagodas in Southeast Asia. Most of the chedis in Thailand, as in Burma, Sri Lanka, and Cambodia, have a greater sense of verticality than the Indian or Tibetan stupas. The chedis of Sukhothai are created from laterite, a building material made of red-colored porous soil, which hardens when exposed to the air.

Even though most of the kingdom has collapsed, the archeologists have done their job. There is a prevailing sense of order and dignity to the space which reflects a unity of architectural design. Most of the chedis are in the shape of a lotus bud, a style invented by Sukhothai artisans during the reign of King Lo Thai. Unlike many chedis or stupas, such as the ones in Borobudur or the three-dimensional mandalas of Tibet, most of these chedis were built to contain Buddha relics brought from

Sri Lanka as well as various Buddha images. However, veneration of the relics themselves is not the main issue; ideally these structures are symbolic reminders of the awakened state of mind and are meant to encourage meditation. Traditionally a pilgrim circumambulates them in the direction of the sun's course. There are no pilgrims here, however, and everything seems too arranged, too protected and overrestored, too much of an archeological museum without any real spiritual substance.

No doubt, though, the alternative to restoration would be disintegration. Twenty years ago, before Sukhothai became a historical park, the unprotected tourist was threatened by bands of outlaws.

I watch Lynn as she stands without moving, contemplating the huge Buddha with its oval head bearing a crown, its face dominated by a serene mystical smile. Perhaps, for a moment, she has found relief and acceptance of a grief that is always with her. The loss of Ayrev has been accompanied by spiritual necessity, as if, for a moment, all of our obscurations that formerly kept us so far from diligent effort dissolved, and we were so naked and exposed that we had no choice but to be aware of a higher Dharmic view, to actually sit down and practice . . . to live with and remember the "four thoughts that change the mind":

The freedoms and the favorable conditions of this human birth are extremely difficult to obtain. Everything that is born is impermanent and bound to die. The results of virtuous and unvirtuous actions are inexorable. The three realms of existence have the nature of an ocean of suffering. Remembering this, may my mind turn toward the Dharma!

At first, after the accident, the only relief was meditation. Twice and sometimes three times a day we would sit in our shrine room at home, sometimes with friends, often alone. Always we would recite the *Prajnaparamita Sutra,* or *Heart Sutra,* the "Great Sutra of Wisdom," culminating with its mantra: OM GATE GATE PARAGATE PARASAMGATE GATE BODHI SVAHA . . . "Gone, gone beyond, gone completely beyond—awakened mind, so be it." The usual distractions fell away, and often I found myself being grateful for this grief, as if Ayrev had, in some poignant way, become our teacher. But now that we're thrust back into the world, meditation has become less spontaneous. Traveling itself has become a distraction, even on this pilgrimage. We are left with a new appreciation of our limitations.

I am still weak and ignorant from the ravages of the night, and after walking around the statues and chedis, almost all of which have collapsed, I find a position in front of a "walking" Buddha, a figure that I had never seen before and whose fluid and flowing attitude of "be-coming" is not, in fact, found in many other periods. This one is positioned on a raised stone platform, its left hand raised in the "attitude of teaching," the thumb and forefinger delicately joined, the right leg stepping forward, the left heel bent in the process.

But it is the elegance of the slightly curving right hand that holds me. Open and yet hesitant, vulnerable and at the same time reflecting the courage of "walking on," the totally relaxed fingers are androgynous, beyond gender, neither coming nor going, but endlessly becoming. Even so, the fingers seem to beckon. They are slightly seductive, tantalizing, inviting. There is none of the stern detachment of Indian or even Tibetan Buddhist sculpture. I look up at the face, at the erect, confident posture of the body. The whole expression, from the delicately turning fingers to the mysterious beatific smile, is one of total equanimity. The figure walks forward as within an illuminated dream. The journey is not revealed, because it cannot be told and cannot appear. It is a "flight through the air" of one who no longer needs to move at all in order to be anywhere.

The movement seems beyond grace. Its aesthetic demands contemplation, a focus that suddenly fills me with shock. The Buddha seems to be walking right through me. It is a levitation that is more than I can assimilate. The *Amitayurdhyana Sutta* is explicit: if you ask *how* is one to behold the Buddha, the answer is that you have done so only when the thirty-two major and eighty minor characteristics of Buddhahood have been assumed in your own heart.

But I can't name these characteristics. I can't recognize or inhabit them. My mind is too ignorant, too cluttered and conceptual, my heart too full of unassimilated closures and weird obscurations. I'm still a "road junkie" looking for sensations, for adventure. Even, God forbid, for entertainment. I can look. I can be thrilled. I can be appreciative. But can I endlessly be?

I close my eyes and open them again. The Buddha is still there but I am somewhere else.

I only looked at one other sculpture in Sukhothai: a seated Buddha in a folded-leg posture, with the right hand hanging down on his right knee and the left palm on his lap. It is the classic pose: Buddha calling upon the earth to witness his enlightenment after subduing Mara, his tempter.

I immediately feel grounded. Mara, after all, is an old friend: my enemy, the ego. The Lord of the Desire Realm who supports my selfishness, my fear of death, my endless self-induced sufferings. Mara is present on this pilgrimage, lurking around, asking for a profound experience, a release from the pain of Ayrev's death, hope for Lynn, even an affirmation of life. Anything but the truth of the present moment.

After Siddhartha defeated Mara and attained enlightenment under the Bodhi Tree, he pointed his finger to the earth as his witness. Is the earth my witness? Do I even have one?

Buddha "goes where no one else will dare." He doesn't travel, although he "walks on" continually. He doesn't look at travel guides or check schedules. He doesn't look for new experiences or new situations. He sits on the ground in the "action of nonaction." Beyond waiting. Beyond becoming. Beyond hope and fear.

> Seeing the frightful transformations of Mara's army,
> The Pure Being recognizes them all as a product of
>   illusion.
>
> There is no demon, no army, no being;
> there is not even a self.
> Like the image of the moon in the water
> the cycle of the three worlds is misleading.
>   —*Lalitavistara Sutra*

On the way back to the van, Lynn says that all morning her camera was on the edge of malfunctioning and that several times she thought the shutter had broken. It was opening on the rewind, which meant that everything would be overexposed. I'm suddenly panicked. She

63

uses an ancient Rolleiflex and has left her backup camera in New York. Now that the Italian-English producer has completely abandoned us, we are dependent on her work for the magazine—not just for the money, but as a *modus operandi,* a reason for going on, for a focus to hang on to and function behind. Now everything is in jeopardy.

"It was strange," Lynn says with a faraway smile. "When it broke, I just stopped and completely gave up. I was ready to never take another picture. And then the shutter just started to work again."

*   *   *

We roll up the road to Chiang Mai. Once known as the kingdom of Lanna, Chiang Mai is the original seat of Thai culture. I've heard about the city for years from junkie friends as an easy place to score the opium and hashish that trickles down from the Golden Triangle.

It is a city that travel brochures boast as justifying Thailand's old sobriquet as the Land of Smiles. These days, however, there is an international airport, highrise condominiums, modern hotels, air pollution, traffic jams, and the worst ratio of AIDS in Thailand. There are not many smiles. In fact, for the three days we are there, it feels as if there is a grim pall over the city.

We are staying at the Chiang Mai Orchid, a modern hotel with a slick lobby complete with coffee shop, fitness center, and restaurant featuring European cuisine. Neither of us feels very well, and yet the hotel is so oppressive that we are driven outside. Luckily, we have set up a trip to visit the Akha, a hill tribe living north of the city near Doi Suthep, the region's highest mountain.

Along the way, the driver stops his Toyota jeep at an orchid farm and snake ranch. The snakes are housed in pits, and the whole display is similar to the rattlesnake ranches in the Southwest, complete with a show demonstrating thirteen varieties of poisonous snakes. This display of poison doesn't hold us. It is too theatrical, too manipulative, and the orchids, even hovered over by hundreds of swooping butterflies imprisoned in large nets, are merely beautiful.

In Buddhist art, at the center of the wheel of life are depicted the "three poisons": a cock (addiction and attachment) chasing a snake (hatred and aversion), which in turn is chasing a pig (delusion, confusion, indifference, identification). When one is consumed with these poisons, nature becomes an object, something to be exploited, to be used for greed, power, fame. Clearly the three poisons are dominating the world. And perhaps just as clearly, the usual Buddhist means of combating these poisons—eliminating the boundary between observer and observed—isn't working. The gods of consumerism are in the ascendancy.

We continue up the road to the mountain. Even from a superficial perspective, the ecology of the region is a disaster. Widespread logging and slash-and-burn deforestation techniques, called swidden architecture, have left huge gaps in the forest. This entire northern region used to be covered by evergreen and deciduous forests. In 1961, 53 percent of the region was still covered by forest, but now the canopy of forest is less than 20 percent. Illegal logging is rampant, and nothing has been done to replant areas that have been stripped of trees.

The forest is vanishing at more than a million acres a year, together with much of the fauna that lives underneath its canopy. The rhinoceros and several varieties of deer are now almost extinct. In fact, most of the large mammals of northern Thailand are nearly gone, including wild water buffalo, tigers, panthers, leopards, and black bears. Monkey populations have been decimated by hunting and from greedy merchants who sell them as pets.

We pass a few rice paddies, which are unexpectedly green, while behind us, most of Chiang Mai is covered with smoke from villagers burning their fields. Finally, the Toyota turns off onto a dirt road, and we travel for a few miles, stopping once at a checkpoint where the guard looks us over. Obviously we're not opium smugglers or illegal loggers, and he lets us through with a tired wave. We leave the Toyota and walk along a narrow path up into the *pah paa*, or open jungle. Soon we arrive at a village of a few dozen raised wooden huts with very low thatched roofs. Underneath are spaces for keeping animals, such as pigs, and tools. It is very hot, and only a few villagers are around. No one pays us much attention as we approach. Obviously tourists have visited before.

Thirty years ago, this particular tribe wandered down from the mountains of Burma after having originally come from Tibet four or five hundred years after the birth of the Buddha. The scene feels like a kind of Disneyland display where the *farang*, or foreigner, is shown how the simple hill people live. We sit down near an elder, an old man in a dirty sarong who takes us matter-of-factly upstairs to sit on a platform which affords a view of the small valley. Underneath us, three young girls, solemn and beautiful, walk from one house to another. Because they are still virgins, they wear white neck-high dresses. I wonder if some of them will be sold to the brothels of Patpong, not an uncommon occurrence in the north.

We offer the obligatory cigarettes and take a few snaps from our Polaroid, offering the prints around.

This causes a small commotion, but it is obviously a ritual they have been through before.

The women wear heavy silver jewelry, and several of them smoke pipes. The tribespeople are supposedly opium farmers, but I see no evidence of any poppy fields.

After sitting around for an hour, there is nothing to do but leave. We aren't anthropologists, and, as we have nothing more to offer, our presence becomes awkward. Self-consciously we walk back through the village and down the path leading to the Toyota. I realize I haven't even asked if they are Buddhists, but our guide tells us later they are animists, although several of the tribes have become Christian.

In the *Dhammapada*, the Buddha says:

> Think clearly, avoid evil;
> Forsake false doctrine, deny the world . . .

But can we deny the world? If Siddhartha were born today and once again he had the choice between becoming a Buddha or a *chakravartin* (a universal monarch), which would he choose? Enlightenment or universal worldly authority? Which choice, given the state of the world, would be the most beneficial? Obviously his teachings expose eternal truths and are thus universal. But the question still occurs: would not an enlightened world monarch be a greater surgeon for the world's ailments than individual methods of realizing nonself, or nirvana?

Given a period of general decline, which we now seem to be in—the Kali Yuga, a phase of plague, famine, and war that has been described as "the end of the end"—what language would the Blessed One skillfully use to resolve the world's demise? In contrast to the physical reality of his own age, nature itself seems now threatened with extinction. If we believe that, what is the significance of meditative practices in the modern world, particularly when the "extinction" clock reads two minutes to midnight? Can we spend our time in seclusion and contemplation—even if, of course, we are not striving only for our own enlightenment but for all sentient beings as well? Is enlightenment more important than saving the world? Or is enlightenment the only way of saving the world?

Thich Nhat Hanh says: "Meditation is not to get out of society, to escape from society, but to prepare for a re-entry into society. We call this 'engaged Buddhism.'"

Buddhism is not concerned just with private destiny, but with the lives and consciousness of all beings. This inevitably entails a concern with social and political matters, and these receive a large share of attention in the teachings of the Buddha as they are recorded in the Pali Canon. Any attempt to understand Buddhism apart from its social dimension is fundamentally a mistake. Until Western Buddhists understand this, their embrace of Buddhism will not help very much in the efforts to bring about meaningful and positive social change, or even in their struggle to transform their ego.

—SULAK SIVARAKSA

It is time for inner city meditators. Time for the Victorious Ones to get their hands dirty in the myriad hell and hungry-ghost worlds of the planet. Time for bhikkus and bhikkunis to understand the addictions of television and the comforts of the corporate state. Time for spiritual warriors to taste the toxic garbage of a collapsing ecology. If there is to be any more "time."

burma

This is Burma and it will be quite unlike any land you know about.

—RUDYARD KIPLING

THE NEXT MORNING we take the morning flight to Bangkok, and then the hour flight to Rangoon, or Yangon, as it's now called, the capital of the amazingly odd and oppressive country of Myanmar, which was formerly Burma.

Even in the airplane we go through a time change. Everyone looks grim and shabby. The service is nonexistent, the plane old and decrepit.

Mingaladon airport is even more antiquated, smaller, and less efficient than those that serve any small city in the United States. A few prop planes and a small one-story building mark the only official entrance to Burma's capital of three million people. Once inside, a mad chaos of passengers push their way past rows of wooden desks, filling out endless forms in triplicate over carbon paper as thin and used-up as dead mosquito wings. A few ceiling fans push the hot, humid air over the shouting mob, watched over by impassive, infuriatingly bu-reaucratic officials.

Luckily, we are met by our tourist guide, Rosie, a calm and pleasant middle-aged woman in a green uni-form who somehow manages to direct us through cus-toms and out the broken door to an ancient 1952 Ford.

As the driver steers the old car out of the airport and down a broad boulevard lined with pink oleander trees, we enter another world, a world exactly the opposite of Bangkok. We almost weep with nostalgia. Only a few ancient cars are on the road, most of them Fords, Chevys, and Hillmans, all of them cruising, like us, at no more than twenty miles an hour. As few as five years ago there were only a couple of hundred cars in Ran-goon; now there are a few thousand, but the streets still seem shockingly empty of transportation, and, most dra-matic of all, there is no noise, no sign of commerce, no industry, and, just as shocking, no tourists.

In the sweet dusty evening we pass men and women strolling slowly about in *longhis* (sarongs), elders loung-ing in front of crisscross mat houses, an old woman leaning against a building smoking a large cheroot, a line of yellow-robed monks walking silently past a circle of giggling schoolchildren wearing black and white uni-forms.

We turn up another broad boulevard, passing decayed Edwardian mansions set behind thick, overgrown gardens, remnants of the British who first conquered half of Burma in 1853, claimed total sovereignty in 1886, and ruled until 1937, when Burma was accorded separate status within the British empire. Finally, in 1948, it was granted total independence.

We have entered a dream, a land without contemporary definition, a place with no high-rises, no television antennae, no glittering Hiltons or Sheratons. Even the washed-out billboards, advertising toothpaste and hand-painted Asian movie stars, are like romantic hallucinations of the fifties.

The old Ford turns a corner. There, in front of us on Singuttara Hill, rising over an awning of trees, is a glimpse of the Shwedagon Pagoda, the top of its stupa shimmering gold in the fading tropical night. According to legend, the pagoda is twenty-five hundred years old and enshrines eight hairs of the Buddha, as well as other relics of previous Buddhas. When the Indian Buddhist emperor Ashoka came to Burma in the third century BCE, he made extensive repairs on the pagoda and cut down the encroaching jungle. Subsequent Buddhist kings all added various improvements until 1768, when King Hsinbyushin had it rebuilt after an earthquake to its present height of 326 feet.

But we are ignorant of these facts, and luckily Rosie

doesn't inform us. We are left to experience the golden spire of the pagoda, without verbal concepts or information, as an essential gesture of spiritual ascendency that points directly to a darkening and empty sky.

Our hotel, the Inya Lake, brings us back to "dependent origins," as the Buddhists say, or mundane relativity. The Inya Lake is a massive block of concrete built by the Russians in the mid-sixties. It has all the charm of post-neo-Stalinist architecture, from the grim receptionists in the wide, empty lobby to the massive, neon-lit ballroom at the end of a long rectangular corridor. Backpackers and hard-core travelers refer to the Inya Lake as "the Bunker."

Our room does not betray the aesthetics of the lobby; in fact, it even enhances it. The decor is pure Southern California fifties motel kitsch. The air-conditioning clanks, issuing out only a hint of coolness, the toilet doesn't work, the strange box in the corner that is meant to serve as a refrigerator is useless. The black-and-white TV offers two national stations that come on at 7:30 P.M. and end at 9:30, always with the same announcer reading a prepared script of censored news, which of course we can't understand because we don't know a word of Burmese. But at this point we refuse to be discouraged. Instead, we are charmed by the whole display, even the sagging double bed and plastic three-legged desk.

Lynn takes a nap while I hang out in the lobby, always a favorite pastime of mine. I sit down on one of the large plastic-covered sofas facing the front door. The lobby is empty except for three Japanese businessmen in identical gray suits looking over the impoverished counter of the tourist shop. They are specifically interested in a row of stamps the Japanese made during World War II when they occupied Burma. There seem to be more Japanese tourists in Rangoon than any other kind. The airport was full of them. Mostly they are elderly, traveling in organized groups in new air-conditioned vans as they tour through India and Southeast Asia, atoning for their buried World War II dead and making organized pilgrimages to various holy places, such as Lumbini and Kapilavastu in Nepal, the birthplace of the Buddha, and Bodhgaya in India, where the Buddha became enlightened, as well as to famous Buddhist shrines in Thailand, Burma, Sri Lanka, and Borobudur in Indonesia.

Two Burmese generals, their chests full of medals, sweep imperiously into the lobby, followed by their two wives, their plump, well-oiled bodies wrapped in purple and yellow sarongs. I'm reminded that the country is under the control of a military dictatorship, the State Law and Order Restoration Council (SLORC), and that only a few miles away, Aung San Suu Kyi is under house arrest.

As the daughter of Aung San, Burma's national hero who helped the country gain independence in 1948, Aung San Suu Kyi entered politics in 1988, after Ne Win, the autocratic general who had ruled Burma since 1962, resigned, throwing the country into chaos. The army quickly staged a coup to solidify its position, and much of the country took to the streets in spontaneous demonstrations against twenty-six years of political repression and economic decline. At the same time, Aung San Suu Kyi, with several associates, started the National League for Democracy (NLD). Inevitably, the ruling junta placed her under house arrest.

In 1990 elections were held, initiated by the head of state, General Saw Maung, who obviously thought the elections would result in a coalition of many parties, which could easily be controlled by the junta. But the opposite happened. Even though Aung San Suu Kyi was still under house arrest, the NLD won over 80 percent of the vote, causing SLORC to decree that Aung San Suu Kyi's candidacy was invalid.

Initially, Burma seems to lend itself to an easy romance of political erosion and decay. How attracted I am to dissolution and even inversion. I feel freer, more at home, when the state of things has collapsed. But that is a privileged external view, this alienation from external order and discipline.

These fat, arrogant SLORC generals, who have now been joined by a dozen more, obviously on their way to a party or reception in the hotel, fill me with a kind of horror. And yet I am fascinated. And this fascination leads, even as I'm sitting in the cavernous lobby, to outrage, and inevitably to feeling myself as separated. It is the opposite of unity, the result of Dharmic truth. I think of the example of the Dalai Lama, who is able to love his enemies, the Chinese, with wisdom and compassion, even as they have killed, with genocidal lust, over a million of his people. I fail even the crudest example of *karuna*, or compassion, with people who aren't even formally my enemies.

Aung San Suu Kyi has given a political overview in her writings:

> Why has Burma with its abundant natural and human resources failed to live up to its early promise as one of the most energetic and fastest-developing nations in Southeast Asia? . . . The Burmese people, who have had no access to sophisticated academic material, got to the heart of the matter by turning to the words of the Buddha on the four causes of decline and decay: failure

to recover that which had been lost, omission to repair that which had been damaged, disregard of the need for reasonable economy, and the elevation to leadership of men without morality or learning.

Translated into contemporary terms, when democratic rights had been lost to military dictatorship, sufficient efforts had not been made to regain them, moral and political values had been allowed to deteriorate without concerted attempts to save the situation, the economy had been badly managed, and the country had been ruled by men without integrity and wisdom.

Of course, the irony is that if Aung San Suu Kyi succeeded in her reforms, it would open the door to those Western poisons Sulak Sivaraksha so eloquently despairs of. No doubt, that is a risk one is compelled to take, but even so, the ultimate result is not necessarily a positive one.

The lobby has filled with even more officers and well-dressed civilians, now slowly moving toward the large reception room in the rear. I flee back to our room.

The next morning we cruise downtown Rangoon. There are a few more cars at the intersections, some of them even new Japanese Toyota jeeps. Rosie tells us this is because every Burmese sailor is allowed to import one vehicle a year, which he then sells off. Now every girl in Rangoon wants to marry a sailor.

The heat is stifling, but the city seems to bend with

it, obliging and passive, like a burned-out old whore. There is no hustle, no urgency, very little traffic. Trees are everywhere, and the wide, shady streets are laid out in a traditional British colonial grid system. "No hurry, no worry," as the Taoists say in their fortune cookies.

We browse through a few bookstores, finding no new books and almost nothing on Burma, and surprisingly little on Buddhism. Most of the stock is eighteenth- and nineteenth-century English novels: Trollope, Dickens, Hardy, Austen—good veranda reading for those nineteenth-century English colonialists trapped inside their compounds in the rainy and hot seasons.

We visit Chauk Htat Gyi Pagoda, which features an enormous, recently built 230-foot reclining Buddha underneath a large half-open structure, somewhat like a railroad shed. Very few pilgrims are about. Aside from its size, the Buddha feels without spiritual juice, its features bland and superficial, as if it has been made for the *Guinness Book of Records*—five feet bigger than the famous reclining Buddha at Polonnaruwa in Sri Lanka.

In any case, it must have cost the congregation a lot of *kyat* to produce it, particularly when one considers that Burma, in per-capita terms, is one of the ten poorest nations in the world.

We seem to be growing physically weaker, as if the heat and strange time warp of this antiquated and willfully stalled country are draining our energy. We retreat to the Strand Hotel, a faded white stucco turn-of-the-century building in the middle of the city that the guide-book promises is on a par with the Raffles in Singapore and the Oriental in Bangkok. In fact, it points out, the Sarkie Brothers, who built it, also were proprietors of Raffles ("the Savoy of the East"). Not only that, but included among its distinguished guests were the Grand Duke Cyril of Russia and William Taft, a former president of the United States, as well as the usual list of old Asian hands: Somerset Maugham, Joseph Conrad, and Graham Greene.

Once again, we are transported into another time zone. Even though a crude wooden scaffolding is set up on the outside of the building for repairs, inside it doesn't seem as if even the deep rattan chairs and cracked leather couches have been shifted as much as an inch since Somerset Maugham clapped his hands for a fresh lime and Mandalay rum, no ice. A ceiling fan barely waves the hot, sticky air over the few tired businessmen sitting at the round tables. A young German couple, obviously hardened backpackers, sit opposite us, counting their kyats and then offering us an exchange for dollars, as they're on their way to Laos and don't want to leave Burma with any local currency, which is virtually worthless outside the country. We make the transaction, gossiping about rumors we had heard in Bangkok about the SLORC treatment of AIDS victims, which is to quickly inject them with cyanide, thus the absence of AIDS in Burma. They tell us about the government's policy of dropping Agent Orange and other lethal herbicides over the agricultural fields of various insurgent tribes, of which there are seven main ones, killing their crops and forcing many of them to flee across the Salween River on the eastern frontier into internment camps located in Thailand. Despite these catastrophic rumors, they love Burma and seem thrilled by the absence of the usual litany of contemporary malaise that afflicts the rest of the world, from consumer madness to overpopulation to pollution and all the "time-saving" devices of fast food, faster transportation, TV reductionism, and the instant gratification of all our appetites. It's a trade-off they seem willing to make, although after their two weeks are up, they will fly back to Germany and resume their middle-class lives in Hamburg, where they run a computer store. Standing up, they salute us and march back into the ferocious heat, on their way to the train station and a third-class trip to Mandalay.

Behind us, a few clerks sit at a row of ancient wooden desks, listlessly typing on huge upright Remingtons. The whole scene reminds me of a Calcutta hotel or one of the old English colonial inns at a hill station in northern India. Another time, another sense of order, all mixed into a surreal display of dilapidated and malfunctioning comfort.

Lynn gets up to go to the bathroom, accompanied by a waiter because the ladies' room isn't working and he has to stand guard in front of the gents' while she goes inside.

I pick up a copy of the *Guardian*, one of two newspapers in Rangoon, the other being *Working People's Daily*. Both are put out by the government, and both are highly censored. My eye falls on a lead article:

Myanmar's military authorities, in a fresh crackdown on Western influences in their country, have been arresting teenagers wearing T-shirts decorated with flags of foreign countries in Yangon, a Myanmar businessman said.

Merchants in Yangon have also been ordered to stop selling T-shirts decorated with pictures of Western heavy-metal rock bands and also pictures of sexy couples, said the trader, who spoke on condition of anonymity.

The T-shirt crackdown includes garments bearing foreign flags, in particular the U.S. Stars and Stripes and Britain's Union Jack, he said. Video cassette rental shops have also been raided since January and Western films confiscated, he said. Some video shop owners had been arrested, he added.

Most of the Western-style clothing and video cassettes are imported from Thailand.

Instead of being amused, I am suddenly overwhelmed, remembering Ayrev and how we used to bring him back exotic T-shirts from such remote places as Greenland, Nicaragua, and western Australia. His collection is still neatly hung up in his closet in our house in Hudson, New York, a house that we bought with him in mind, that he could always use as a refuge as he found his own way in the world.

So far, we haven't had the courage to give his T-shirts away to his friends. It is as if we are afraid that once his clothes and objects have disappeared, an essential part of him will also be removed. Part of the purpose of this pilgrimage, if that is what it is, was to raise our view, to surrender all these lingering attachments and join our personal suffering to a larger grief: the grief of the world, where millions of children die every day, where someone is killed in a car crash in the U.S. every twelve minutes, and finally, unalterably, where one lives at ease with the truth that "everything born is impermanent and bound to die."

Lynn comes back, and we have a Burmese-Chinese lunch of mushy overcooked vegetables and potatoes, which sink to the bottom of our stomachs like leaded gruel. We drive back to the hotel to rest up for a visit to the Shwedagon Pagoda, the reason we came to Rangoon in the first place.

In the cool of the evening, we take off our shoes and walk up the covered steps to the Pagoda. On either side of us, small shops sell flowers for offerings, Buddha images, incense sticks, and religious books and antiques. It is dark underneath the covering, the crowd pleasantly subdued, the air smelling of jasmine and sandalwood. The long upward passageway has a curious effect. It seems to calm us, to prepare us in some way, as if with each step we discard more of our conceptual minds and become one with the gentle crowd walking up and down the steps. Every move, every gesture and sound around us, becomes slower, as if part of a collective ritual, so ancient that its progressions are without religious vanity or self-consciousness.

We step out of the darkness. In front of us, the gilded pagoda rises up from the bell shape of the lower stupa (Buddha's inverted begging bowl), its glowing ascendancy surrounded by a cluster of smaller pagodas, statues, and *tazaungs* (shrine buildings).

We have entered a magical Buddha world, a community and promenade of pilgrims and worshipers where everything seems included, from circumambulating monks to businessmen making deals, to entire families chatting and eating snacks, children running in circles, old men and women dozing, astrologers offering advice, tourists gazing and looking in their guidebooks, silent meditators, sleepers, students reading, debating, all ages hanging out, walking, shuffling, prostrating, skipping, musing, contemplating. Just being. Around it all, laughter, bells, and resounding gongs, bird song, monks chanting. It is like an enchanted village that the gods have blessed. And above, holding it all together, is the giant stupa with its 28,000 packets of gold leaf which are redone every ten years, and the *hti*, or umbrella, at the top hung with gold, silver bells, and jewels, all chiming and jingling in the illuminated air. The whole embrace of this sacred space is childlike, innocent, and profoundly, endlessly vast.

We join the dreamy crowd, walking clockwise around the giant circle on gray and white marble tiles, cool now in the night air. I feel, for the first time on this trip, that I am inside a living refuge, a place of the spirit where every thought, every passion, every emotion becomes an offering; a place where all the grief of the past months, the pain and abandonment, the fear and even the exhilaration of total gut-wrenching loss is received, as if from an impersonal and yet profoundly intimate embrace.

Lynn stops to stare up at the pagoda. To her photographer's eye, the relationship between the sky and the spire of the pagoda represents an equal division of positive and negative space. But which is positive? she wonders. Which is negative?

Lights come on, a display of candles, bulbs, neon, and technicolor diffusing gently with the brightly colored red, purple, yellow, green of the Burmese *longhis* and the glittering shrines and statues, all resonating from the central golden display of the pagoda.

Despite all the activity, everything is quiet and harmonious. No separation between keeping still, stopping, pausing or moving on. Noise has become silence, movement has become stillness, speech has become prayer.

Lynn wanders off with her camera, too dazed to really focus on any object. I sit in front of a glittering shrine hall dedicated to Konagamana, the second Buddha.

With each inhale and exhale I feel myself slowing down. All the brittle mental speed, the endless distractions, the compulsive informational devices, the increasing acceleration of my "time-filled" world spins out of its manic journey toward inevitable entropy and becomes, for a moment, a spiral toward renewal.

I don't even think of a relevant quote, such as from the *Suttanipata:* "He who abstains from interfering is everywhere secure." I don't even think of Ayrev or Lynn. I don't even think. And then, of course, I do think, and I'm looking for Lynn and wondering what she's photographing, and I'm checking out an old white-bearded Chinese pilgrim muttering to himself and slapping his head in some kind of weird *kriya*, or spontaneous gesture, and the world filters in after this "pause for bare attention."

> If you analyze time very precisely, there is no present, in the real sense of the word; only past and future, no present! The sense of present that we have is a conventional notion. Even if you employ a computer or some other instrument to divide time and analyze whether there was a present or not, you would find that there isn't. "Present" is a relative term. While in experience there seems to be nothing but the present, we actually experience only the illusion of the present.
>
> —Tenzin Gyatso,
> THE FOURTEENTH DALAI LAMA

*   *   *

Lynn is growing weaker. She might even be seriously sick, from a combination of heat, nightmares, bad food, and exhaustion. But she is determined to press on, knowing that to stop right now would mean abandoning the rest of the trip. We have one more day in Rangoon, and after another visit to the Shwedagon Pagoda, we ask Rosie if we can visit a monastery.

The monastery Rosie chooses, the Chanmyay Yeiktha Meditation Center off Pagoda Road, is only ten minutes from our hotel. It consists of several three-story buildings set around a small courtyard. Immediately upon entering, there is a sense of diligence and calm. We stand outside a small office while Rosie goes inside to ask if we can have a brief audience with an English-speaking monk. In front of us, descending down an outer staircase, we notice a parade of young girls, teenage novices wearing pink robes. Their eyes are lowered; each movement, each step is considered. Their concentration is ferocious. Later on, I copy the walking meditation instructions from a little booklet on *vipassana* meditation by the Venerable Sayadaw U Janakabhivama, the abbot of the monastery.

Take the walking meditation seriously. By merely doing walking meditation, one can reach Arhat-ship! [The state of an *arhat*, one who gains his own salvation, the highest level of the Hinayana]. Take the Venerable Subhadda, the last Arhat disciple of the Buddha, as an example.

Bring your attention to the foot during walking meditation. Note the movement with sharp awareness. At the beginning, note the step in one part only, mentally note "right" and "left."

Do not close your eyes but keep them half-closed, looking ahead about four or five feet.

Do not bend the head too low. This will cause tension and dizziness in a short time.

Do not look at your feet. Your mind will get distracted.

When you follow the movement of the foot, you must not lift the feet too high.

The objects to be noted are increased gradually; that is, the number of parts of a step that are observed is gradually increased.

Later one may watch the step in one part for about ten minutes, followed by three parts "lifting," "pushing," "lowering." Finally it may be further increased to: "intending," "lifting," "pushing," "lowering," "touching," "pressing."

Please consider this—within one hour of walking meditation, the mind is sure to wander off quite a few times.

You must not look around here and there during walking meditation. You have had and will have many years to look around. If you do so during the retreat, you say goodbye to concentration. Take note of the "desire" to look around. The wandering eye is a very difficult problem for a yogi.

At least five to six hours each walking and sitting meditation per day is recommended.

Not one of the girls looks up or notices the passage of the Westerners as they "walk" slowly past.

After a long wait, Rosie comes out of the office, and we take off our shoes and follow her up to the second floor of a white stucco building. We pass several rooms.

In one of them, half a dozen Western monks sit quietly on mats. They have freshly shaven heads and are all alarmingly emaciated.

They look at us dispassionately, without curiosity, not projecting the impression of spiritual superiority that one usually receives from Western monks or "inside" students when visiting a monastery in the States, or, for that matter, in other parts of Asia. In fact, they are too dazed and absorbed to notice us.

We stop in front of a spare reception room at the far end of the balcony. Inside, a monk gives an audience to a young novice who seems quite agitated. Even though this monk is somewhere in his late twenties, he obviously holds a position of authority. He is erect and handsome, with a Chinese cast to his high-cheekboned face. As he talks to the young novice, his gaze is stern and direct.

He motions for Rosie to enter. We wait at the door while she tells him that we would like to speak with him. He glances briefly at us, then addresses the young novice, whose entire body seems to be trembling. "He wants to leave the monastery," Rosie whispers to us. "He's having trouble with his mind."

Finally the novice, who apparently has been given permission to leave, bows and backs out of the room. The monk motions for us to approach. As we walk into the room, he gestures for us to sit in front of him. He looks at us sternly. In perfect, distant English he tells us that one has to observe the 227 precepts, or rules of conduct knows as *patimokkha*, in order to become a member of the Sangha. The schedule is from 3:30 A.M. to 10:00 P.M., and basically the practice involves labeling every gesture: "I am breathing in. I am breathing out. I am writing. I am intending to sit. I am sitting. I am intending to take a step. I am taking a step. I am feeling anger. I am feeling pain. Like that."

He pauses, sipping tea. "I will give you an example of how we practice with the mind. Without any wishing or wanting to come here, can you come here?"

We look at him blankly. After a pause, he questions us again.

"What is the cause and what is the effect? The act of coming is the effect, the intention the cause. Why are you sitting on the floor? It is attention that makes you sit on the floor. Is there any sitter? If you think there is a person who sits on the floor, then we should bring a corpse from the hospital and make it sit on the floor. It cannot sit because there is no intention. It is only intention, the mental process, that causes an action or movement. So who is sitting now? A man or a woman? Neither. It is a physical process supported by wind. That is why we have to observe intention before every action."

Finally he smiles and asks us where we are from. When we tell him the United States, he asks if we know Jack Kornfield, the American *vipassana* teacher. We shake our heads. We have heard of him and read a book of his but have never met him.

"He has been here," the monk says. "He has very good students. I would like to go to America and visit him, but no one is allowed out of Burma."

I ask him if he is Chinese. He smiles and nods his head. His parents were both Chinese who lived in Rangoon, where he was born. There are a lot of Chinese in Rangoon, he explains. Indians also.

I tell him about Ayrev and that we have come to Burma on a pilgrimage as well as to various other holy places in Thailand and Cambodia.

He nods, his eyes suddenly compassionate. "We never know the moment of death. It is so important to realize that every phenomenon is subject to impermanence. Your son has died. Any one of us here in this room can die at any moment. There is great suffering when we do not fully realize the instant arising and passing away of mental and physical phenomena."

He looks at his watch and abruptly stands up. He has to officiate at an ordination. Would we like to come?

We follow him down the stairs and across the courtyard to another building. A small crowd has gathered inside a large green reception room. The furniture looks like it belongs in the lobby of a Holiday Inn in Topeka, Kansas, circa 1950. The abbot, an elderly man with thick glasses, sits on a couch with white doilies on the arm rests. In front of him, kneeling on the floor, are two middle-aged men dressed in the stiff, newly bought white robes of novices. Behind them, also on the floor, are their families, perhaps fifty people in all.

Rosie explains that they are a ship's captain and his first mate and that next month they will both marry girls from Rangoon. Before the marriage, however, they are committed to doing a ten-day retreat in the monastery.

The Chinese monk, who is obviously used to this sort of ceremony, leads them through their vows, which they receive kneeling on the floor, their hands pressed together in front of their chests. As laymen, they vow to obey eight precepts: abstaining from killing, stealing, sexual misconduct, telling lies, and using any kind of intoxicant or eating food after noon. The seventh precept is refraining from dancing, singing, playing music, or adorning yourself with anything that will beautify yourself, such as flowers or perfume. The eighth precept is abstention from a high and luxurious bed.

The abbot, who seems gently bored, nods occasionally and offers further explanations. After the captain and his first mate have finished their vows, he explains that when the eight precepts are fully observed, their moral conduct will be purified. The purification of *sila,* or *sila-visuddhi,* is the prerequisite of a meditator to make progress in his meditational practice. When *sila,* or moral conduct, is purified, one never feels guilty. When one does not feel guilty, one's mind becomes steady. Then the mind can easily focus on the object of meditation. Purified moral conduct leads to deep concentration of mind, which, in turn, gives rise to insight wisdom in one's meditational practice.

Everyone has tea, and the abbot has an attendant pass around snapshots of his trip to Japan, where he visited Mount Fuji, several parks, and quite a few monasteries.

On the way out of the monastery, I stop in front of the office where the daily meditation schedule is posted.

TIME	PROGRAM
4:00 A.M.	Wake up
4:30 A.M.	Walking
5:30 A.M.	Sitting
6:30 A.M.	Walking
7:00 A.M.	Breakfast
8:00 A.M.	Walking
9:00 A.M.	Sitting
10:00 A.M.	Walking
11:00 A.M.	Lunch
12:00 A.M.	Rest
13:00 P.M.	Sitting

14:00 P.M.	Walking
15:00 P.M.	Sitting
16:00 P.M.	Walking
17:00 P.M.	Juice served
17:30 P.M.	Walking
18:30 P.M.	Sitting
19:30 P.M.	Walking
20:00 P.M.	Dhamma lecture
21:30 P.M.	Sitting
22:30 P.M.	Private meditation

After a last visit to the Shwedagon Pagoda, which we can never seem to get enough of, we drive by Aung San Suu Kyi's house on University Avenue, a few blocks away from the American consulate. Five uniformed guards stand on the street outside the locked gate of the two-story wooden bungalow. Even driving by, Rosie seems afraid to look, as if the ever-present SLORC will somehow notice and document our interest.

How long will Aung San Suu Kyi be interned? Has she accepted the bitter situation of her country? Obviously not. More to the point is whether she has maintained compassion for her country. Has she, in her mind, run away to the past or future? Is she walking, standing, sitting with mindfulness? Perhaps the power to stay where one is without argument or complaint is to be in touch with a deeper rhythm. Perhaps it is the "action of nonaction."

I'm reminded of a statement by the Dalai Lama:

> One thing that influences my outlook is that if in any situation there is no solution, there is no point in being anxious. The forces at work have their own momentum, and what's going on now is the product of what went before, and if this generation is not in control of all those forces, then this process will continue. . . . If there is trouble, some understanding brings a benefit from it. Life becomes useful when you confront a difficulty; it provides a kind of value for your life to have the kind of responsibility to confront it and overcome it. Whereas if you do not feel such difficulties, there's no such responsibility, no role for you to play in your life. . . . That challenge allows you to practice your ability. Basically, the purpose of life is to serve other people. From that point of view, a difficulty is really a great opportunity. I have often said that our generation of Tibetans is seeing the saddest part in all of Tibetan history. So from that angle it is . . . a great *honor*, a great privilege . . . to face these times, to confront them.

*   *   *

Early the next morning we take a small plane to the ancient ruins of Pagan near the Irrawaddy River. The plane flies over green jungle, lakes, rivers and fields. From the air, Burma seems unspoiled, as if it has somehow escaped the toxic and murderous disasters of the twentieth century.

On the ground, however, it is another reality.

The small airport is empty except for a few soldiers lounging outside the one-room terminal. Apparently we are the only tourists on today's flight, which is understandable, as the heat almost rocks us backward as we walk toward our jeep accompanied by Kyi Kyi, the young woman who is our guide. Kyi Kyi, whose broad face is covered with *thanaka*, a light brown sandalwood paste used to prevent sunburn, is glad to see us, as the tourist trade has been slow, if not practically nonexistent. Even though she works for the government tourist agency, which is one of the best jobs in Pagan, she makes ten dollars a month, not much when you have a few kids to support as well as an alcoholic husband.

On the way to the hotel, we stop in front of a small, partially collapsed pagoda standing at the edge of a field. Tufts of grass grow over the pagoda's three receding terraces. On top, the finial has spread across the bell-shaped stupa like a mushroom as the entire shape slowly descends into the earth, a process that began over nine centuries ago.

While Lynn shoots, I wander across the dusty overgrown field. Around us, on the vast plain, are a scattering of pagodas and temples, part of several thousand that are left from a religious city that included over thirteen thousand stupas and temples and seventy thousand monks, as well as a university which was equal to the great Nalanda University in India. The whole Buddhist succession of kingdoms lasted only a few hundred years.

"What happened?" I ask Kyi Kyi.

She sighs. "What always happens. Everything disappeared."

Now, aside from the ruins, there are only a few poor villages left, which until recently included Kyi Kyi's own village, which for hundreds of years had existed in the same place within the temple grounds. But recently the government forced the entire village of five thousand people, who were noticably pro–Aung San Suu Kyi in the 1990 elections, to move to another site, all to be done within four days. By removing the last village of Pagan, SLORC turned the site into an archeological museum: sterile, safe, and lifeless. Now only pagodas and temples are left, as all other structures, including the king's palaces, were made of wood.

Behind the pagoda, an ox cart slowly moves across a dusty field. There is no other movement, no other sign of life. And soon the ox cart is gone as well.

While Lynn photographs the pagoda, Kyi Kyi gives me a brief history lesson: the first Buddhist king was Anawrahta (the Burmese spelling of Aniruddha), who ascended the throne in 1044. The eleventh and last was Narathipati, who became known as "the king who fled from the Chinese" when he tore down ten thousand buildings in 1287 to defend the empire against a threatened Mogul invasion by Kublai Khan.

After that, it was over. The hills were eroded and treeless after two hundred years of compulsive building. The food and water supply could no longer support a large population, and when the Tatars rode in to sack the city, nothing remained.

Kyi Kyi tells me the story of Anawrahta, obviously a favorite part of her repertoire of Buddhist king stories, some of which have all the brutal and violent dimensions of the *Ramayana* or the *Mahabharata*. Anawrahta's conversion to Theravadan Buddhism was initiated by a learned monk sent to him by Manuha, the Mon king of Thaton. Apparently Anawrahta had a fairly large number of obscurations to dissolve and sins to atone for, including the killing of his half-brother, the preceding king, Sokkade, in man-to-man combat. But the monk was so successful in his conversion that Anawrahta asked Manuha for a number of sacred texts and relics, including thirty-two copies of the Tripitaka scriptures (the essence of Buddhist religious writings).

Manuha, however, was suspicious of the quality of Anawrahta's response. How could such a self-important king be so easily won over to the Theravadan scriptures? Anawrahta must have another, baser motive.

When Manuha refused the request, Anawrahta immediately declared war and conquered Thaton, bringing back to Pagan not only the Tripitaka but the city's monks and architects and even King Manuha himself.

As if to prove his conversion was real, Anawrahta immediately engaged in a frenzy of building which not only continued after his death but for roughly two hundred years, until it burned itself out.

> The Buddhist view of kingship does not invest the ruler with the divine right to govern the realm as he pleases. He is expected to observe the Ten Duties of Kings, the Seven Safeguards against Decline, the Four Assistances to the People, and to be guided by numerous other codes of conduct such as the Twelve Practices of Rulers, the Six Attributes of Leaders, the Eight Virtues of Kings and the Four Ways to Overcome Peril. There is logic to a tradition which includes the king among the five enemies or perils and which subscribes to many sets of moral instructions for the edification of those in positions of authority. The people of Burma have had much experience of despotic rule and possess a great awareness of the unhappy gap that can exist between the theory and practice of government.
>
> — AUNG SAN SUU KYI

As for Manuha, his destiny was to become an architect as well as an exiled king. As we continue on to the hotel, Kyi Kyi points out the temple that Anawrahta

allowed Manuha to spend the rest of his life building.
Despite the heat, which is well over a hundred degrees,
we stop. From the outside, the temple is not impressive.
It is an uninspired square structure with the upper level
smaller than the lower, as if Manuha somehow had in
mind a pyramid but did not have the aesthetic confidence or belief in spiritual ascendancy to really
achieve it.

Inside we find out why. In front of us, in a small
cramped passageway, we encounter three large seated
Buddhas and a reclining Buddha. They are much too
large for the space. The effect is violently claustrophobic, as if they have been confined to a prison.

Kyi Kyi explains that was the intention. The positions
of the Buddhas represent the physical discomfort and
stress that Manuha felt in captivity. The reclining Buddha, with a beatific smile on his face, represented for
him the final longed-for release of death and the only
possible end to his suffering.

If you don't have the basic framework of *shunyata** and
egoless practice of meditation, then it would be a pa-

---

*Shunyata, or emptiness, is a central teaching of Buddhism. An-
cient Buddhism recognized that all composite things are empty, impermanent, devoid of an essence, and characterized by suffering.
Shunyata does not mean that things do not exist but rather that they
are nothing but appearances.

thetic gesture to try to appoint yourself king and not quite make it.

—CHÖGYAM TRUNGPA, RINPOCHE

Violence is totally contrary to the teaching of Buddhism. The good ruler vanquishes ill will with loving kindness, wickedness with virtue, parsimony with liberality and falsehood with truth.

The Emperor Ashoka, who ruled his realm in accordance with the principles of non-violence and compassion, is always held up as an ideal Buddhist king. A government should not attempt to enjoin submission through harshness and immoral force but should aim at *dhamma-vijaya*, a conquest by righteousness.

—AUNG SAN SUU KYI

Lynn asks Kyi Kyi how a Buddhist country like Burma can be so violent and brutal over so many centuries. And how can the present government accept responsibility for killing so many people?

Kyi Kyi shrugs. "Because they get non-Buddhist tribal people to do it for them. No problem."

*   *   *

We are staying at the Thiripyitsaya Hotel in a little bungalow. It is supposedly the best hotel in Pagan, if not the whole country, and by Burmese standards it probably is. There is a refrigerator in the room that is almost cool and a ferocious clanking blast of cold air from the AC. The toilet works except for a busted handle. The faucet in the sink continually drips, but water eventually does emerge. No problem. Outside the door, the temperature is over a hundred and fifteen degrees.

The rest of the hotel includes a bar and a veranda that looks out on the Irrawaddy. But the lobby feels oppressive, perhaps because of the large amount of unfriendly SLORC lurking in the restaurant, or hanging around their Toyota jeeps in the driveway. When the SLORC are around, all of the waiters and staff are particularly obsequious and at the same time distant, as if they are unsure of what the correct attitude is when dealing with Westerners.

After lunch we collapse, waiting for evening before we venture out again.

* * *

We climb to the top of Thatbinyu Temple, the highest building in Pagan, built by King Alaungsithu (1113–1160). After climbing a narrow, claustrophobic flight of stairs and passing a huge Buddha image, we finally emerge on an upper terrace. Beneath us, bathed in an orange and crimson sunset, stretches the flat plain of Pagan. We can see hundreds of temples and pagodas, most of them in decay. Further away, the Irrawaddy bends in a great sluggish curve, empty except for two wooden barges gliding slowly toward Mandalay.

A wave of futility overwhelms me. Why are we here? Is it just to see or witness these monuments to impermanence? Are we just collecting and cataloguing sacred images that will soon disappear like dreams?

The buildings are only external shells, empty of spiritual juice. I feel empty as well. Not empty in the profound Mahayana sense of abandoning fixed notions or realizing that voidness includes everything; rather, empty of substance, of wisdom, of the "big view" of nonduality. It is as if we are on a pilgrimage to nowhere, coming from nowhere, going nowhere. Not a bad state, actually, if we are living truly in the present.

But dissatisfaction gallops through me. Our journey has been nothing more than an insane kind of visual materialism, a precarious prop to cover up our grief. What is the point of distinguishing this temple from that pagoda or finding that Thai sculpture is more ornate and decorative than the Cambodian or Indian? We cannot be soothed. We cannot be nourished. Only the compulsive hardships of this journey seem to distract, and even those for not very long. What is the point of knowing that this temple was built as an atonement for some hideous murder or that one out of remorse or competition or self-aggrandizement? Despite the massive pile of bricks beneath us, I feel as if I am floating helplessly, foolishly in the air. And then, helplessness suddenly turns to hopelessness. Immediately I feel stronger and weaker. Because this pilgrimage is, in fact, hopeless, and there is some relief in acknowledging that. Ayrev is gone. In a blink, Lynn and I will be gone as well, and just as this kingdom has vanished, Buddhism, too, will vanish. None of it is a big deal. There is no guilt and no blame. And no fear, either.

On the other side of the terrace, Lynn is staring, transfixed, at the Ananda Pagoda, the setting sun shining off its white graduated terraces and golden spire. A soft smile plays across her lips. She has no need to photograph. Only to look. Only to be. She turns to me, radiant, ecstatic. My mad little mental dance dissolves as suddenly as it arose.

On the way back to dinner, we stop in front of the Ngakywenadaung Pagoda, a forty-three-foot round stupa shaped like a bulbous cylinder. Part of the pagoda is still covered with green glazed tiles. The shape holds us by its simplicity, as if it has arisen spontaneously from the earth, not designed, not formed, not preconceived. Its presence transmits everything that is potential, that will arise and unfold. It is the womb and lingam joined, possessing a presence more profound than mere beauty.

It has no obvious cultural aesthetic, no conceptual meaning. It is nothing less than the pulsating shape of existence, a statement that has no beginning and no end.

The next day we journey out again in an orgy of pagoda and temple gazing. The dream of this religious city begins to permeate us. What must it have been like to be totally surrounded by Buddha Dharma, to live in a community that was, for the most part, dedicated toward the evolution of the human psyche? Perhaps there were hundreds, even thousands of realized beings living here, teaching, meditating, transmitting. Is it possible that at one time a culture could exist without consumerism, without worldly manipulations or ambitions, without even the idea of progress? Of course, the three poisons are always present, but perhaps their antidotes were available as well.

Perhaps . . . but we have no antidote for the heat, and retreat back to the hotel.

Each relationship is energy. The concept of sangha, for instance, means a group of people working together as brothers and sisters, working together as spiritual friends to one another. . . . In order to be spiritual friends you have to be open to each other. . . . Being open is not being dependent on others, which blocks *their* openness. In other words, the sangha does not create a situation of claustrophobia for each person in it. If somebody falls, you still stand independently; because you are not leaning on the other person, you don't fall. When one person falls, it doesn't create a chain reaction of other people falling as well. So independence is equally important as being together, acting as an inspiration to one another.

—CHÖGYAM TRUNGPA, RINPOCHE

As the jeep turns down the dirt road toward the hotel, a crazed figure wearing shorts, backpack, tank shirt, and red bandanna over a trail of long wispy hair, passes us on a bicycle, swaying from side to side in buffeting waves of heat. We go another fifty yards before we realize that it's Michael Wadleigh! We make a plan to meet for dinner, and Wadleigh bicycles back to his guest house, where he is camping underneath a small half-tent and mosquito net.

After a restless nap, we have dinner with Wadleigh, surrounded by groups of SLORC sitting glumly with their families. Since we last saw Wadleigh in Bangkok, he has been traveling the low road through the Burmese countryside, sniffing out information in Rangoon for a film about Aung San Suu Kyi, hanging out on trains and buses, singing songs with the exotic boat people of Inye Lake, climbing the 1,729 steps to the top of Mandalay Hill, only to find posters of Madonna and the Terminator flanking a wall painting of the Buddha, and having a series of eccentric adventures that make us feel, by comparison, pathetically overprotected and indulgent. But we get over that reduction quickly. Three days on the road Wadleigh-style and we would be sent back to the States in body bags.

In a loud voice which all the SLORC can hear, Wadleigh describes various attempts to get to Aung San Suu Kyi, all of which failed. One meeting with a U.S. official, probably CIA, particularly incenses him. The official didn't see any reason to let Suu, as Wadleigh refers to her, out of confinement. She would only cause trouble. But of course, if she did somehow take over the country, she couldn't be counted on to perform well, as no woman could effectively rule an Asian country. Wadleigh also said that the "gray suit," in a moment of candor, admitted that the United States, despite officially suspending aid to Burma, gives them hundreds of millions under the table to keep the junta alive, part of a deal for gas and oil rights.

By this time the waiters are avoiding our table and the SLORC are staring sullenly at their plates. Wadleigh tells us that a man came up to him at his guest house asking if he could mail a letter for him out of the country. Apparently the man, who lived in a neighboring village, had already spent a few years in prison for some minor infraction and was trembling with fear.

Wadleigh said he would be glad to act as a courier and made plans to meet him the following night, but the man never showed up. He had disappeared without a trace.

All the SLORC and their families stand up at once and file out of the room, not looking at us.

*   *   *

The night before we are to leave for Rangoon, the electricity goes out. The windows don't open. If we go outside, swarms of mosquitoes eat us alive. It is so hot that we can barely breathe. We are trapped in a tomb, at the mercy of the failed mechanisms of progress. All night we think of Wadleigh sleeping peacefully underneath his mosquito net.

The night has left us wretched and sick, both of us with hacking coughs. Lynn has trouble breathing, and her heart feels as if it's slowing down. After saying goodbye to Wadleigh, who is going off to Rangoon by bus for a last try at finding some documentary footage of Aung San Suu Kyi, we spend the rest of the day looking at monuments.

We begin by visiting the Shwesandaw Pagoda, the first monument built by Anawrahta after returning from his conquest of Thaton, which is said to contain some sacred hairs of the Buddha. Then we stumble into a low red brick building, thinking it might contain monk cells or perhaps wall paintings.

Totally dominating a low-ceilinged rectangular room is a reclining Buddha. The figure is sixty feet long, about the width and length of a sperm whale. The head points to the south rather than the north, the traditional position assumed by Buddha when he was lying on his deathbed between two sal trees at Kushinara.

The light is very dim, and as we stand in front of the huge figure only a few feet in front of us, we feel diminished and insignificant. The black hair is coiled, the smile serene and infinitely tender and wise in its acceptance of death. But it is the position of the feet, with the left foot resting gently on the right, that express an almost unbearable vulnerability and intimacy.

We sit down on the dirt floor. It is cool and there is no sound at all. The rest of the world has disappeared. We sit without speaking for a very long time.

Finally, Lynn stands. She takes a small package from her purse and approaches the face of Gautama Buddha. A small flower offering has been placed near the open right hand. She removes a small pile of ashes from the package: the remains of a picture of Ayrev that we burned after the traditional forty-nine days of mourning. She places the ashes next to the flowers along with a copy of one of the last poems Ayrev wrote.

Ah kindred spirit
Fellow man
What seek we two against forces of infinity?
Deities,
Take us to the ends of the earth
(or we shall take ourselves)
Warriors
Searchers
Caressing the sand with open eyes
You and I
We walk our paths together
And apart

To celebrate our last night in Pagan, we take a boat down the Irrawaddy, passing the white Bupaya Pagoda with its rows of crenellated terraces. Women and children bathe near the shore. Farther away, a group of monks wade knee-deep in the shallow water. An old man leads an ox cart into the river, filling up a large wooden barrel with water—a scene that has repeated itself for thousands of years.

> The hulks of ancient river boats floating down to Mandalay.
>
> —SOMERSET MAUGHAM

The next day we fly back to Rangoon, and then to Bangkok for an overnight stay before we fly on to Cambodia and the sacred ruins of Angkor Wat and Angkor Thom.

On the plane to Bangkok, Lynn's heart slows down, even skipping beats. Her headache is worse, and she has a fever. Several times she feels as if she's about to faint. She can barely keep her head from slumping over. While I hold her hand, trying to control my concern, I skim through a few Thai newspapers.

Two former U.S. Congressmen said five prominent Burmese dissidents they visited in jail yesterday appeared in good health.

It was the first time the country's military junta had permitted foreigners to visit jailed dissidents. In a brief interview with the Associated Press, the former Congressmen said the prisoners appeared healthy and said they spent their time meditating.

United States stopped aid to Burma in 1988, after soldiers killed hundreds, if not thousands, of civilians in a coup that installed the junta.

No outside officials have been allowed to see the most prominent detainee, Nobel Peace Prize laureate San Suu Kyi. Mrs. Suu Kyi is in her fourth year of house arrest in Rangoon. Her party won parliamentary elections but has not been permitted to take power.

As we board the bus to take us to the terminal, Lynn sags against me, holding my arm. We are in another in-between state, or *bardo*, another rehearsal, perhaps, for the "final event."

Sogyal Rinpoche writes:

One of the central characteristics of the bardos is that they are periods of deep uncertainty. . . . As the world around us becomes more turbulent, so our lives become more fragmented. Out of touch and disconnected from ourselves, we are anxious, restless, and often paranoid. . . . to live in the modern world is to live in what clearly is a bardo realm; you don't have to die to experience one.

Lynn looks up at me, managing a smile, as if she's trying to reassure me. "I am glad to be here," she whispers. "Really. I don't want to be anywhere else. Everything is perfect."

cambodia

IN THE LONG CUSTOMS LINE at the Bangkok airport, Lynn has trouble standing up and leaves the line to sit against a nearby wall, joining a small boy in a Toronto Blue Jays baseball jacket, who is sitting cross-legged on the floor, holding his head in his hands. In the Rangoon airport we had made friends with the boy's father, a farmer from British Columbia. Several months ago his wife had died of cancer, and he decided to take his son on a trip with him to Thailand and Burma. The son, who is eight years old, has been sick for several days with a stomach virus and has already thrown up twice in the airport bathroom. Now he and Lynn sit together holding hands. A mother without a son and a son without a mother.

Finally, after two hours in line, Lynn joins me and we clear customs. We barely have the strength to make it to the airport hotel.

I want to immediately cancel our trip to Cambodia, but Lynn insists on going on. Our room seems to have revived her. It is in the style of a Hilton or Holiday Inn, with a well-stocked refrigerator, cable TV, plenty of hot water, even room service. We are back in the modern world of CNN and Hollywood movies. Larry King is interviewing Henry Kissinger on the situation in Bosnia—another country disintegrating into anarchy and ethnic strife. I remember Kissinger and Nixon when they initiated the bombing of Cambodia in 1973 in an effort to stop the communist forces from taking over Phnom Penh, an effort that was finally stopped by Congress against the bitter protests of the president. That year over a hundred thousand tons of "foreign aid" rained down from the sky, killing countless peasants and no doubt strengthening the resolve of the communists, who finally, in 1975, marched into the city, many of their troops no more than fifteen years old. And then came the worst interlude of all, when Cambodia became Democratic Kampuchea under the leadership of Pol Pot, a reign which was responsible for the massacre of over a million innocent people. The terrible "hell world" came to an end when Vietnam invaded in 1979, occupying the country for ten years, until the spring of 1989.

> The [Pol Pot] revolution swept through the country like a forest fire or a typhoon, and its spokesmen claimed that "over two thousand years of Cambodian history" had ended. So had money, markets, formal education, Buddhism, books, private property, diverse clothing styles, and freedom of movement.
>
> —DAVID P. CHANDLER, *A History of Cambodia*

We order chicken soup and club sandwiches and try to watch Dustin Hoffman in *Hook*, falling asleep after twenty minutes.

In the morning Lynn's fever is down. Despite my persistent misgivings and fears, we decide to take the plane to Phnom Penh. We seem to be locked into movement for its own sake, as if by constantly changing the outside we will in some way encourage a realization within of the truth of impermanence. But we need desperately to stop traveling, to drop anchor somewhere, anywhere. Lynn's grief is more than I can even imagine. It is as if part of her has died as well.

The relationship between mother and son must be the most profound, the most biological, and the most shattering when it is brutally ended. We go on because to stop is to be surrounded by hallucinations, to lose control, to constantly see Ayrev's body lying on the gurney in the Phoenix hospital. The otherworldly stillness of his face, the deep purple bruises around his empty eyes. Lynn gently lifting the sheet covering his body. Externally, the body has not been damaged. Lean and hauntingly graceful, it is a body that has never known decay or the ravages of time. Mercifully, the young intern was brief and to the point: "He fell asleep at the wheel. He never knew what hit him."

An internal chant while waiting for the plane to

Phnom Penh: Let go of grief. Let go of joy. Let go of hope. Let go of fear. Let go of history. Let go of coming and going. Let go of culture. Let go of waiting. Let go of letting go.

*   *   *

The Phnom Penh airport is pure chaos, totally unlike the surreal control of Rangoon or the modern international efficiency of Bangkok. In the oppressive, drenching heat, everyone is shouting, waving forms, paying off duty taxes, grabbing suitcases. There are no tourists. Only UN officials, Cambodian soldiers, and a few businessmen.

We take a cab to the Cambodiana, a large French hotel on the Mekong River. The influence of the French is everywhere, from the large, well-laid-out boulevards to street cafés and pastry shops. The city feels frayed and exhausted, as if poised for another invasion or civil war. Prince Sihanouk is once again supposed to be in charge, but he is still hiding out in China. And yet, for a moment, we feel comfortable here. In the sixties, at the height of the Vietnam War, Phnom Penh was a favorite city for American soldiers on R and R. Now there are no Americans anywhere. The hotel is almost empty except for a few officials and their families bathing in the large pool outside, which affords a spectacular view of the massively broad and curving Mekong River.

We are too tired to tour the city or pay a visit to the museum, which hosts a display of thousands of human skulls—a reminder of the Khmer Rouge's orgy of genocidal lust, which resulted in the death of over a million Cambodians between 1975 and 1979.

Where was I and what was I doing in those years? Writing a book, a few film scripts in between a failed love affair, hiding out in New Mexico, studying Dharma in Nepal, surviving in New York. Drugs, sex, and rock 'n' roll. Trying to meditate. I can't remember the lineup.

In the bookstore off the lobby I pick up a copy of the *Nation*, the daily Bangkok newspaper. The center section is almost entirely devoted to Cambodia.

Cambodia is a mess. Nobody seems to be in control. As the planned May elections draw near, the election campaign is expected to increase the already volatile atmosphere. Violence can be expected to escalate as the 20 contesting political parties take up their positions and try to woo supporters.

A campaign of brutal attacks by the Khmer Rouge against Vietnamese settlers in the past few months has now moved to the cities, especially Phnom Penh. Savage assaults are being directed at Vietnamese-owned restaurants, shops and other establishments. . . . Because of the ferocity of the Khmer Rouge attacks and

123

the rising death toll, UNTAC has had to take a more assertive role in guaranteeing the safety of the Vietnamese.

We sleep the rest of the day, content to look out at the Mekong, which is empty except for a few fishing boats.

The next morning at breakfast, before our flight to Siem Reap, more news in the paper about Khmer Rouge atrocities:

> Three Khmer Rouge guerrillas dined pleasantly with UN peacekeepers before opening fire at the end of the meal and killing three Bulgarians in what the United Nations called a "cold-blooded" execution. The method was reminiscent of Khmer Rouge purges during their years in power between 1975 and 1979, when cadres considered to be traitors were recalled to the capital for "meetings," then feted with banquets and gifts before being surprised with execution at the end of the meal.

If the three poisons of samsara, the passions of worldly suffering, are greed, hatred, and delusion, one could see Thailand as greed, Burma as delusion, and Cambodia as hatred. Certainly we seem to have entered a hell world.

> Basically, hell seems to be related with ultimate aggression. Aggression that is based on such perpetual hatred that you begin to lose the point. You are uncertain as to whom you are building up your aggression toward, or

by whom your aggression is being built up. There is
that continual process of uncertainty and confusion. Not
only that, but you begin to build up a whole environment of aggression around yourself.

. . . It is as if you are walking in a hot climate. You
yourself might feel physically cool, but at the same time
you begin to get this hot air coming at you constantly.
So you cannot keep yourself cool . . . because the environment creates heat. . . . There is no space to breathe
in and there is no space to act.

There is no space to move at all. The whole process
becomes overwhelming. . . . Whatever you see around
you is hot and intense, stuffy, extremely claustrophobic.

CHÖGYAM TRUNGPA, RINPOCHE

*   *   *

The flight to Siem Reap takes an hour in a small
plane. There are about twenty passengers: a few French
tourists, the rest Cambodians, including an ancient
white-robed nun, the first official Buddhist we have
seen. There is no air-conditioning, but the pretty flight
attendant glides up and down the plane as if she's part
of a tourist commercial.

It is about twenty degrees hotter and much more humid in Siem Reap, the temperature hovering around a
hundred and ten degrees. When the Vietnamese occupied the region, their troops cut down huge tracts of

forest, taking the lumber back to Vietnam or selling it to the rapacious Thais. This clear-cutting caused the temperature to rise ten to twelve degrees, a disaster for the local agriculture. Outside, the terminal is surrounded by UN troops, and as we walk toward our guide waiting outside near a van, it feels as if we've entered a war zone.

Our guide, Samban, is a small, thin man in his twenties. He seems strangely removed, as if he is just going through the motions with us. When I ask him about the Khmer Rouge, he nonchalantly admits that they have been "causing a little trouble" lately, but there is nothing to worry about as long as you don't walk away from the paths leading to and around the temples. Sometimes, at night, the Khmer Rouge plant land mines and trip wires attached to grenades.

We pass a convoy of UN troops riding in white Toyota jeeps and then a Union Jack flying outside of a ramshackle two-story building, the Mine Field, which serves as a bar for UN troops. The UN presence is everywhere. A few days ago twenty-six Cambodians were killed by the Khmer Rouge, and security is tighter than usual.

The Bangkok *Nation* has more to say:

Suspected Khmer Rouge guerrillas killed 26 people and wounded 20 in a rifle and rocket attack on a village video hall in central Cambodia on Wednesday night, a UN official said.

It was the third massacre within three weeks believed to have been carried out by the radical faction. All the villagers were ethnic Khmers and unarmed civilians.

Agence France-Presse adds:

Suspected Khmer Rouge guerrillas shot from the shore at a group of Vietnamese boat people fleeing their ethnic cleansing campaign, injuring a little girl, a UN spokesman said yesterday.

The gunmen fired from the same shore in Kompong Chang province from where suspected Khmer Rouge guerrillas shot dead or hacked to death eight Vietnamese fishermen last week.

Siem Reap has the run-down, desultory air of a frontier town, which, in a sense, it is. We are staying at the Ta Phron Hotel, since the French hotel we had initially booked is now without water. The Ta Phron is a white four-story building across the street from the polluted Siem Reap River, which runs through the center of town. Small children bathe in the stagnant water, apparently unconcerned that over 40 percent of the population of sixty thousand sooner or later come down with malaria.

There are no phones or public transportation in Siem Reap, and the electricity is constantly going off and on.

Our hotel is clean and subdued and even has a small restaurant that serves French, Cambodian, and Chinese food. Amazingly, there is a TV in the room, which, when the electricity is on, has a BBC Asian news station, now almost entirely devoted to the situation in Hong Kong between the British and Chinese.

After lunch, Samban takes us to Angkor Wat, the largest religious monument in the world. The first European to "discover" Angkor Wat was an eccentric French botanist, Henri Mouhot, who stumbled on it by accident in 1860. His journal, which later became a sensation in Paris, is full of romantic ravings about finding a monument equal "to the temple of Solomon and erected by some ancient Michelangelo." But neither Mouhot nor the few Englishmen who wandered by at that time saw anything particularly spiritual in the ruins. Basically they were cultural materialists, more involved in how big the place was and who could have built it. There was a lot of speculation that the Romans or even Alexander the Great was responsible. Anybody but the Cambodians, whom they considered primitive, congenitally lazy, and decidedly inferior.

Mouhot died a year later in Laos up on the Mekong River, a victim of fever. A recent theory proposes that Angkor Wat was abandoned in the fourteenth century because of an outbreak of malaria caused by the giant reservoirs and irrigation systems, which, when they began to dissipate, turned into stagnant breeding pools. Perhaps Mouhot's fever was malarial and originated from these same pools.

We drive alongside an enormous half-empty moat two and a half miles long where water buffalo lie in the muddy water surrounded by clusters of thick hyacinth. We stop in front of a bridge or causeway guarded by two stone lions leading to a massive display of pavilions and stone towers: Angkor Wat, the City Temple.

Nothing moves in the dense heat. A few beggars stare vacantly at us as we walk across the bridge, which seems wide enough for an army or a parade of elephants. Halfway across, we pass a crippled musician sitting underneath a statue of a hooded cobra, or *naga*, a classic Hindu water deity. The musician plays two melancholy notes over and over on a Cambodian violin. The dirgelike sound follows us, as if we were approaching an empty fortress of forbidden secrets and obscure rituals.

> The Khmer kingdom has gone, as all empires go, as all our brief human existence must go.
>
> —PAUL BRUNTON

The architectural design of Angkor Wat is based on the five peaks of Mount Meru, an ancient Hindu cosmological idea of a "world mountain" standing in the center of the universe and surrounded by seas and continents. The moat would be the ocean, and the surrounding enclosures would be the mountains which enclose the central continent, dominated by Mount Meru. Strangely, the entrance is from the west, contrary to most temples, which face east. This has given rise to various theories that Angkor Wat was built as a tomb as much as a temple.

Inside the outer wall, which is pockmarked with bullet holes, a different spatial proportion consumes us. It is like being enveloped in the mechanism of a huge esoteric clock, only we are unaware of what time it is or what calendar is being followed. We are forever outside the inner workings of the Angkor Wat mandala, unaware of the generosity of its ancient transmissions or even of its cruelties. All we have is travel information and history books and a dull litany of facts from our guide, all of which seem, when confronted with the actual presence of Angkor Wat, to be totally inadequate.

> The close fit of these spatial relationships to notions of cosmic time, and the extraordinary accuracy and symmetry of all the measurements at Angkor, combine to confirm the notion that the temple was, in fact, a coded religious text that could be read by experts moving along its walkways from one dimension to the next.
> — DAVID P. CHANDLER, *A History of Cambodia*

Our own subjective sense of time has collapsed as well. We barely know the day or even the month. Lynn seems to be proceeding on will alone, as if by insisting on the role of a professional photographer, by covering the site from every angle, she can somehow find the strength to go on. It gives her strength even as it debilitates her. Hour by hour she is growing weaker. Her gaze, which is constantly measuring space and light, is beginning to turn inward, sliding into an endless spiral of memory and grief.

We stumble around the massive solemnity of this tomb, or temple mountain, which offers not so much solace or refuge as it does awe and even a shiver of atavistic fear at the omniscience of its precision. It is a place of power, a city of the dead, once ruled by Hindu *devarajas,* or god-kings, under whose totality religious art and sculpture reflect Shiva and Vishnu as much as Lord Buddha. Giant lingams, stylized phalluses, exist side by side with statues of the Buddha and endless bas-reliefs of the *Mahabharata* and *Ramayana.* One huge bas-relief in particular stuns us with its fluid elegance in depicting the Hindu creation myth, "churning the sea of milk." In a union between gods and demons, the giant serpent Vasuki is pulled back and forth between the monkey god, Hanuman, and a line of demons. Vasuki, who has wrapped himself around Mount Mandara, is supported by a giant turtle in the Sea of Milk, the ocean of immortality. As Vishnu oversees this divine rhythm of opposites, the gods and demons rotate the mountain and churn the sea into foam, releasing a seminal fluid which creates a divine ambrosia, or *amrita*, the essence or elixir of life. Much of the bas-relief has faded from centuries of worshipers rubbing their hands over the figures, but overall it is still exquisitely defined.

Lynn stands transfixed before the forces of the underworld and the celestial gods, at the divine play of life and death. Lately Lynn has been making her own journeys into the underworld in an effort to subpoena the dark forces, willing to make any deal to bring her son back to her. And yet, as she disappears into the darkness of anger, frustration, and grief, the light is gathering. The serpent is being stretched. The sea is boiling.

She moves off to photograph the giant stone stairs, which seem not so much to ascend the main pyramid as to prohibit ascent. I stand off to the side, thinking of the line of Khmer kings whose reigns seemed to shift so easily from Hinduism to Buddhism and back again. All of them built their monuments with slaves and were surrounded by a hierarchy of priests, merchants, and peasants, a system which, on the surface, seems similar to the class structure of ancient Egypt and the Mayans. Suryavaram II, who built Angkor Wat as a monument to himself in the twelfth century, was a devotee of Vishnu. He was preceded by Suryavaram I, who, even though a Hindu, encouraged Buddhist scholarship. After his death, Suryavaram II was succeeded by Dharanindravarman II, a fervent Buddhist.

It is this unselfconscious mix of Hinduism and Buddhism that gives Angkor Wat its peculiar singularity. But this abundance of religious and heroic narrative surrounded by massive verticality is finally too busy, too formal to absorb, as if Suryavaram II, in his inclusion of religious power and politics in this monument to himself as *devaraja*, compromised the experience of emptiness inherent in spiritual attainment.

In 1296, a Chinese diplomat, Chou Ta-kuan, offered a description of the excessive pageantry of Khmer courtly life:

When the King leaves his palace, the procession is headed by the soldiery; then come the flags, the banners, the music. Girls of the palace, three or five hundred in number, gaily dressed, with flowers in their hair and tapers in their hands, are massed together. Then come more girls, the bodyguard of the palace, holding shields and lances. . . . Ministers and princes, mounted on elephants, are preceded by bearers of scarlet parasols with numbers. . . . Finally the Sovereign appears, standing erect on an elephant and holding in his hand a sacred sword. This elephant, his tusks sheathed in gold, is accompanied by bearers of twenty white parasols.

A rifle shot splits through the dense air from the surrounding jungle, bringing me back to the present and the Khmer Rouge, who have no problem killing Buddhists or Hindus alike, or, for that matter, the odd tourist or UN observer.

Lynn is standing in the shade of a half-enclosed balcony. Behind her, a bas-relief cut into sandstone displays a grotesque assortment of beings struggling through the tribulations of hell. Some are being devoured by tigers, while others are in the process of being flayed and decapitated by demons. Above her rises a towering temple, massive, unforgiving, a withholding fortress rather than a refuge for tired pilgrims.

Another shot rings out. This one closer.

"Shooting birds," Samban mutters nervously. "Soon no more birds will be left. Like the monkeys. The Vietnamese killed all the monkeys for food. Now there is no food left in the jungle. Like the trees. The Vietnamese cut down all the trees and sold them to the Thais."

As we drive back to the hotel, Samban tells us that the Vietnamese are hated in Siem Reap. The day before, the Khmer Rouge killed thirty-six Vietnamese living in a village by the Mekong River, part of a push to drive all Vietnamese settlers back across the border. He shows me last week's *Phnom Penh Post:*

> The massacre of unarmed ethnic Vietnamese of Phum Chong Kneas on the Tonle Sap in Siem Reap province came as no surprise to U.N. naval observers in the area or to the villagers themselves. In fact, the attack had been expected for a month and U.N. officials in Phnom Penh informed. But the U.N. and the victims were powerless to prevent it according to both sources.
>
> U.N. human rights chief Dennis McNamara described the massacre as "a tragic repetition" of the atrocities carried out by the Khmer Rouge between 1975 and 1979 and pledged to step up U.N. patrols.
>
> But the chief of Siem Reap's U.N. naval observers, Capt. Gary Boyd, said last week they are unable to protect the Vietnamese from future attacks. The villagers, who had their own guns confiscated by State of Cambodia (SOC) officials when UNTAC arrived promising peace, have now fled in terror.

Samban is terrified of the Khmer Rouge. In a sweet, strangely detached voice, he tells us about the Khmer Rouge who occupied Siem Reap after the civil war. They killed all the lawyers, engineers, accountants, and other professional people, including his father, who was a teacher. The Buddhist monks were given a choice to either take off their robes and work in the fields or be executed. A surprising number chose execution.

135

*　　*　　*

We sleep fitfully through the rest of the afternoon. I wake up not knowing where I am. Across from me, Lynn is asleep, bathed in sweat. I feel her forehead. She is running a high fever.

Angkor Wat has overpowered as much as inspired me. It is as if I've trapped myself by wishing for relief, for a transcendent moment, or even, on a more banal level, a catalyst that would revive our sagging energies. The magnificence of the sheer mass of Angkor Wat, the weight and abundance of imagery, has become oppressive. Walking around its walls, underneath the shadows of its temples, I feel crushed by the gravity of religious ambitions. There seems to be no compassion in the dictates of Angkor Wat's demands. The geometry of its design asks not so much for a surrender of the self as for a laying down of arms, a surrender of worldly ambitions, an allegiance to a greater power, as if no one can compete with such a display of magnificence.

I'm disoriented by so much visual grandeur, by how thoroughly the temples and entire complex have resisted the extraordinary collapse of everything else in this desperate country. Not only that, but I suspect I have a case of sunstroke.

Scrawled on a torn piece of paper by the bed, a memo to myself:

I have reached the end of something. Some definition of self that has always hung on my psyche like a crusted barnacle. Why will I not admit that compassion originates directly from the experience of no-self? My belief in the validity of self or ego is insidious and habitual in its endless exploitations, promoting a nihilist shuffle that has always been seductive for me in a tricky, infantile way, as if by reaching out for the end, any kind of end, the end of any known, is to embrace a stale nothingness that offers a temporary comfort and worldly authority, as if from a drug, the sweet seductive zero of heroin or opium, the totality of death, the worldly authority of negation. And then the inevitable rebound toward the hope of a beginning. Toward a belief in the sanctity of the "new." But there is no old and there is no new, and beginning and ending is it itself an illusion.

Nihilism means becoming caught within each temporary circumstance of relative truth and believing in its reality, so the perception of substance seems real.

—THINLEY NORBU RINPOCHE

Grief will do that to you. It will embrace you with despair, it will crystallize suffering as if suffering is somehow a more honest state of mind than transcendence or equanimity. Grief will offer focus and mindfulness. It will seduce you into being receptive to the greatest teachings. Grief and the abyss of loss have made me long for empowerment and refuge, and when this longing inevitably falls away, the danger is numbness and spiritual fatigue. In the twilight of fading grief, the seductive pimp of nihilism will once again appear, smiling from the doorway like an old friend who knows the power of negation and spiritual narcissism, the greatest trap of all. Hooked on pain, on the terror of impermanence, on nothingness, hooked on the demolition of loss. And when the opening into a greater truth doesn't hold and old habits rush forward to reclaim their suffocating space, the mind, or my mind, at any rate, continually reaches out for more information, more adventure, more identification. Not to mention the loopy signature of a personal language which would pin each moment into an illusion of words.

Even though Ayrev is constantly with me and I constantly experience his loss, so much of the pain is a realization of Lynn's pain, an awareness that her loss is beyond anything I have ever experienced. Once Lynn said that giving birth was like creating a connection between two hearts, hers and the one connected to her son. Now one of her hearts has stopped and she is faced with jumping beyond the habits of her dualistic mind to a larger heart, beyond hers, beyond Ayrev's. It is a necessity that I long for, this all-or-nothing leap beyond the conceptual self, and yet all I am left with is the dull beating of my own heart, the sour taste of frustration, and a mind that has trouble with the simplest truth, such as that suffering and pleasure are the same.

> All this doing has no more meaning than walking
>> around a desert,
> All these efforts make my character rigid,
> All this thinking just reinforces my delusions.
> What worldly beings consider to be Dharma is the cause
>> of binding myself.

> All this exertion produces no result,
> All these ideas bring not a single actualization,
> All the numerous wants will never be fulfilled.
> Abandoning activities, may I be able to meditate on the
>> oral instructions.

> —DUDJOM RINPOCHE

Nihilists never believe that consciousness and circumstances arise through karma created by habits planted in *alaya*, the basis of mind. They think that consciousness is completely dependent on substance, and that when death occurs and the circumstances of substance vanish, mind also vanishes. . . . By thinking that mind exists only because of substantial phenomena, it is not recognized that substantial phenomena only exist because of mind.

> —THINLEY NORBU RINPOCHE

I step into the bathroom to take a shower, but no water comes out of the faucet.

I have fallen away from a sense of urgency. All my little words are little thoughts, and all my little thoughts have become little words. I've been unconsciously riding this gift of grief for months, and now I feel abandoned to my obscurations, ill equipped to realize that I have become as attached to my suffering as I have to my pleasures.

One who has clear and direct vision, stirred to a sense of urgency *(samvega)* by things which are deeply moving, will experience a release of energy and courage enabling him to break through his timid hesitations and his rigid routine of life and thought. If that sense of urgency is kept alive, it will bestow the earnestness and persistence required for the work of liberation. Thus said the teachers of old:

This very world here is our field of action.
It harbors the unfoldment of the holy path,
And many things to break complacency.
Be stirred by things which may well move the heart,
And being stirred, strive wisely and fight on!

— NYANAPONIKA THERA

* * *

We are too tired and sick to experience the evening light of Angkor Thom. The bronchial cough I picked up in Pagan has deepened, and Lynn's fever refuses to go away. But the next morning, after a night of violent dreams, Samban drives us to Angkor Thom, the sacred site that pulled us to Southeast Asia in the first place. After Ayrev's death, Lynn became haunted by a picture she saw, in a book on Eastern architecture, of four stone Buddha faces carved into the south gate of the Bayon Temple at Angkor Thom. The half-closed eyes and enigmatic smiles of the Buddhas seemed to promise, with an almost divine humor, an awareness and acceptance of suffering. And, indeed, this religious city built by Jayavarman II in 1181 resonates with images expressing the Mahayana ideals of wisdom (personified by the goddess Prajnaparamita), compassion (the Buddha Lokeshvara), and enlightenment (Shakyamuni Buddha).

We walk toward the giant gate, passing on one side giants *(asura)* and angels *(devata)* pulling the body of two huge snakes. On the other side is a row of Buddha heads. Several of them are missing, and Samban stops to inspect an empty space. The head has been freshly sawed off. "They're stealing them all the time," he informs us. "Across the border in Thailand, thieves get three or four hundred thousand dollars for one head."

The *Bangkok Post* gives a further report:

The latest statue to disappear from Cambodia's Angkor temples had been in the courtyard of a modern palace, 200 metres from a police station.

The statue had survived 1,000 years of tropical weather, the hammers of 19th-century European souvenir hunters and decades of war and turmoil in Cambodia.

The statue, as tall as a human and weighing more than 100 kg, had been stolen the night before from the courtyard of Prince Norodom Sihanouk's northern palace.

The rare 9th-century piece, a female divinity who had lost her head to a previous generation of plunderers, had been in the courtyard only since January.

In the same week, five stone heads were reported stolen from the northern gate of Angkor Thom temple.

On February 10th, 50 armed attackers on motorcycles stormed through Siem Reap shooting rockets and assault rifles, broke into the conservatory and stole 11 pieces the U.N. authority in Cambodia says could be worth $500,000 on the open market.

Siem Reap police chief Colonel Chea Suphat said his force did not have enough men or resources to effectively fight theft from Angkor.

"In a country where there is no law, where the population is ignorant of new laws and doesn't know the history of religion or the local customs, they don't know about preserving precious monuments. What to do," he said.

I wonder if my old friend Orin has a few of these heads already stashed in his back room in Bangkok. It seems that looting and pillaging are one of man's primary instincts. The act of simply watching and observ-

ing—*shamatha-vipashyana*, the development of peace
and insight—is too much to ask for. Better to rip off a
few Dharma teachings and transplant them back to
Western soil than to erase a country's heritage.

Inside the Bayon, all thoughts of contemporary and
historical strife cease. Even our own ailments, which
are severe, seem suspended. Inside the walled city, we
are surrounded by dense silence. The silence leaks into
us, permeating the stones and thick corridors. Above,
in claustrophobic profusion, rise fifty-four towers, each
adorned with four Buddha heads, each smile, each gaze
different, and yet somehow the same, all of them reflecting the wisdom gaze of compassion. The faces are
personalized, as if Jayavarman, as a *dharmaraja*, imposed his own singularities on the more abstract fact of
the Buddha. Underneath, covering the thick walls from
top to bottom, are bas-reliefs depicting the daily life of
Jayavarman's reign. Unlike the bas-reliefs of Angkor
Wat, which are concerned with Hindu myths, these
carvings show a concern for the common people. A stele
to the king reads: "He suffered more from his subjects'
infirmities than from his own, for it is the people's pain
that makes the pain of kings and not their own."

No one seems to know why Jayavarman's kingdom
disappeared, although two hundred years later there are
records of Siamese Hinayana invasions that sacked

Angkor Wat and massacred Mahayana priests. It is intriguing to speculate on the inner collapse of the Mahayana. The reasons for its disintegration might have been more intimate than mere war or conquest. Perhaps it was Jayavarman's own singularity and pride that secreted the seeds of his kingdom's destruction, as if by adopting the role of a "living Buddha" he created a vulnerability greater than his own kingly power. As a *dharmaraja*, he must have been acquainted with the texts of Nagarjuna, the father of Madhyamaka Buddhism, who, when asked why he was destroying all the propositions of his opponents, replied: "There are no propositions. The only real proposition for a Buddhist is to dismantle propositions." Such is the romantic power of Angkor Thom that it is possible to imagine that Jayavarman had reached such a mystical level of realization that he consciously dismantled his own kingdom, thus abandoning himself to the acceleration of a higher law. In any case, whatever the downfall of this Mahayana ideal, even the greatest *dharmaraja*, Ashoka, emperor of India during the third century BCE, could not escape the realization of worldly impotence at the end of his life:

Who now could deny the saying of the Blessed One that "All fortune is the cause of misfortune"? Truth-speaking Gautama asserted that, and indeed he was right! Today, I am no longer obeyed; no matter how many commands I think of issuing, they are all countermanded just like a river that is turned back when it dashes against a mountain cliff." [Again he added:]

> Once he ruled the earth
> under a single umbrella of sovereignty,
> destroyed the haughty enemy of hosts,
> consoled the distressed and the poor,
> but he lost his support,
> fell from his position,
> and today this wretched king
> no longer rules in glory.

> Just like an aśoka tree
> when its flowers are cut off
> and its leaves have shrivelled and fallen,
> this king is drying up.
> —JOHN S. STRONG,
> *The Legend of King Aśoka*

Standing inside the Bayon, we are stunned and buffeted inside these echoes of impermanence. And yet finally they comfort rather than alarm, as if the acknowledgment of one's own death in some way heals the wounds suffered from the passing of others.

I can see Lynn drifting across an elevated balcony above me, passing the only tourist we have seen, an old white-bearded man in a Panama hat filming the ruins with a super eight. And then they both are gone. I think of the strange awkward steps that brought me to this point. Who knows when this journey started. No doubt, before I had even heard the word *Buddha*. The shards of my own spiritual wanderings rise up inside me like secondhand hallucinations. The drugged-out trips of the sixties that led me to Sufi dancing; Hindu chanting; new age enneagrams; Taoist breathing; Gurdjieffian and Arican "stop" exercises, Kriya, Hatha, Siddha, Raja, and Kundalini Yogas, Indian ashrams; analysis; Peruvian and Native American shamanism—and the reverse: cynicism and despair, the deluded excesses of Hollywood, exploiting the intimacies of the psyche under the brightly colored banner of entertainment. Failing to help exorcise the demons of America. In fact, increasing them. Then numbing solipsism rescued by the road again. Life dances on. All the journeys becoming forgotten dreams. And then, finally, haltingly, the Dharma and taking refuge with Dudjom Rinpoche. Followed by twenty more years of traveling. India. Nepal. East and West. L.A. New York. Greenland, Australia, and Peru. North and South. Cape Breton and Nicaragua. And always, in between, banging around the States with Dharma caravans. Sitting, practicing, failing to practice, being initiated into tantras and sutras, exposed, transmitted, empowered to inner secrets and revelations beyond my comprehension. Saying prayers, whispering prayers, yelling prayers, sleeping through prayers, dropping out, coming back, leaving again, hanging in, taking and breaking and retaking vows, burned out by Dharma centers and Tibetan politics. Why? Why not? And who cares? Above me, right now, is the gaze of two hundred Buddhas cut into stone. Cut from their own experience. Cut from nothing, going to nothing. And who is the watcher, who the watched? The *Heart Sutra* says it better:

> O Sariputra, a son or daughter of noble family who wishes to practice the profound *prajnaparamita* should see in this way: seeing the five *skandhas** to be empty of nature. Form is emptiness; emptiness is also form. Emptiness is no other than form; form is no other than emptiness. In the same way, feeling, perception, formation, and consciousness are emptiness. Thus, Sariputra, all dharmas as emptiness . . .

And then there is the death of a twenty-one-year-old boy, a boy who was exploding with creativity and energy. And then he was gone. Like so many others his

---

*A *skandha* is one of the five "aggregates," which constitute the entirety of what is generally known as "personality." They are form, sensation, perception, mental formations, and consciousness. These aggregates are frequently referred to as "aggregates of attachment," since craving or desire attaches itself to them and attracts them to itself; thus it makes of them objects of attachment and brings about suffering.

age. As we will be. Perhaps today. Perhaps tomorrow. "Everything born is impermanent and bound to die."

Once again, I am on my knees, body and arms extended, asking for refuge, bowing to the Buddha's enigmatic smile.

I think of the Venerable Khenpo Karthar Rinpoche's response to a question about his own life:

> I am really a very fascinating person—you know, bald head, pot belly, not knowing a single word of other languages, walking like an old dog, pretending that I am somebody else, trying to put myself in a higher state, and wearing the mask of Dharma. That is my story.

In the late afternoon, we visit Ta Prohm, another temple complex of Jayavarman's, built in 1186 in honor of his mother and Prajnaparamita, the goddess of wisdom. Near the walled entrance a shouting voice from a blaring loudspeaker asks for contributions toward rebuilding a local monastery. They have a long way to go. We are so tired that we can barely move. And yet we press on as if only by witnessing all the temples of Angkor will we finally be able to rest.

Inside Ta Prohm, all is chaos and disintegration. The jungle has invaded the walls and archways. The roots of strangler figs and banyan trees, like giant pythons or octopuses, have split apart the massive slabs of rock of entire temples, strangling images of gods and demons alike, obscuring corbeled archways and corridors in a profusion of twisting tentacles. Now the wisdom of Prajnaparamita belongs to nature and the inevitability of change, erosion, and decay. It is what we face ourselves and what we have come all this way to reaffirm: the futility of not accepting our own mortality. We are not so much haunted by this ruinous display as relieved. There is nothing to do, nothing to wish for, nothing to be afraid of. We need only to let go and surrender to a higher rhythm of causality.

We sit down in the shade of a crushed wall. It is unbearably hot and humid. There is no bird song, no monkey chatter. A bat flying out from underneath a portico is the only sign of life. Lynn is so exhausted that, for the first time, she is unable to photograph.

> When the inhabitants fled from endangered Angkor, the city deserted by men began to be inhabited by Nature. White ants, dampness, and heat gradually destroyed the wooden homes which survived the invader's fires. Finally, vegetation wrestled with stones and won. The leafy bo-tree, octopus-like, a yard in girth, creeps slowly to certain victory over most buildings in Ta Prohm, insinuating its ashen-white paper-thin roots between stones and around columns. They grow, extend, and thicken into masterly and handsome rulers who hold the structures in their grasp.
>
> —PAUL BRUNTON

We struggle on through the ruins, Lynn walking in a daze toward a huge stone lingam while I drift across the rubble of a courtyard. Turning a corner, I almost bump into two young monks in ocher robes leaning against a headless statue of Lokeshvara. The monks are idly chatting with two French tourists lounging on top of a broken stone slab. Both Frenchmen, who seem vaguely stoned, have their heads wrapped in red bandannas. The older of the Frenchmen passes a lighted cigarette to one of the monks, who inhales deeply and passes it to his friend, who, in turn, takes a deep drag. Giggling, he whispers something to a brightly colored parrot perched on his wrist. The Frenchmen are in the middle of a discussion about André Malraux, who, as a young man in the twenties, went to Cambodia with his wife and tried to steal Khmer sculpture from Bantai Sarei. Malraux was busted and had to use all of his connections to keep from going to jail. The monks smile pleasantly, not having heard of Malraux. Nor do they seem particularly upset about the recent pillage of Buddha heads from Angkor Thom. I think of my recent proposal in Bangkok to make a film about Malraux's adventure. It could just as easily be done today, thus avoiding the cost of a period film. A contemporary caper picture ravaging and exploiting the soul of religion, with inevitable karmic results.

I slide away, leaving the Frenchmen to finish their discussion, which has turned to the price of Swiss watches on the black market. Michael Freeman and Roger Warner, in their 1989 book on Angkor, briefly detail the history of thievery in Khmer sculpture:

> Western interest in Khmer sculpture rose (during the Khmer Rouge regime) as pieces—mostly heads, which are easier to carry—began to cross clandestinely into Thailand. After the Vietnamese invaded in December 1978 and overthrew the Khmer Rouge regime, anarchy prevailed and the sculpture trade on the black market flourished. We met more than twenty convicts who had been caught stealing from the temples and who were serving between six and twenty years in Siem Reap prison. They were by no means the first thieves. The tradition of looting goes back to the sacking of Angkor by the Thais, who removed many statues before 1432. (Some of them were later taken by *their* conquerors, the Burmese, in 1569, eventually ending up in Mandalay.) In 1873 Delaporte unashamedly removed many of the finest statues for the cultural enrichment of France.

Lynn and I, each in our own way, are ripping off images and Dharma experiences and bringing them back to the reductive shredder of our own culture. It is up to us to assimilate and transform these experiences, not to exploit or showcase them.

I wonder what will happen to these two stoned monks

who seem to have abandoned all their external codes or vows of behavior. If the Khmer Rouge take over Siem Reap again, will they go with the flow and abandon their robes, or will they face death and the promise of rebirth with the calm acceptance that seems to arrive with confidence in the "view"? Somehow I think they have been contaminated enough by the West and the anarchy and collapse of their own culture to choose survival, at least of the quick-fix variety. It wouldn't surprise me if they ended up in a Cambodian expatriate rock 'n' roll band in Berlin or as art smugglers in Bangkok or Boston.

I find Lynn leaning against a smashed statue of a goddess. She is so weak and faint that immediately I ask Samban to take us back to the hotel.

*   *   *

In our room, Lynn collapses with a severe headache and fever. Lying underneath a sheet, she remarks matter-of-factly that her heart is slowing down. When I put my thumb and forefinger on her wrist to feel her pulse, there is only a faint, irregular beat. I should take her to the hospital, if, indeed, there is a hospital in Siem Reap, or to the UN compound outside of town. They must have a doctor there, even if he's Bulgarian or Pakistani. But she refuses, shaking her head. No hospital.

No doctor. It's as if she has to strip down to the bone of her own necessities, without help. And I'm too exhausted and burned out to convince her otherwise. My entire body aches, and the racking cough that has been with me since Pagan has moved lower into my chest. We lie next to each other, holding hands, numb, vaguely hallucinating as the room closes in around us. Outside there is Siem Reap, a doomed town inside a destroyed country that is rushing toward anarchy and civil war. And beyond that there is Burma and Thailand and Vietnam and China. And beyond that . . . Is Lynn's heart broken or sick? Or both? Or are we just suffering from heatstroke and exhaustion? We have entered a land that we have no map for.

Suddenly, the air-conditioner and the lights go out. We lie on the bed, unable to speak, paralyzed inside an airless box. Finally, helping each other dress, we stagger outside.

All the lights in Siem Reap have gone off. Across the street, a few men have gathered by the antiquated hotel generator. Sitting on car hoods, they inspect it from a distance, as if at any moment it might explode. The night air is cooler. On the street, bicycles glide past under the light of a half-moon hanging up in the sky like a whore's earring. Did we really go to Angkor Wat and Ta Prohm and the Bayon? When was that? Yesterday? Last year? Three hundred years ago? A thousand years ago? Did Shiva and Vishnu really dance with the deities of the Mahayana? We have walked on the bones of the Khmer past, but its empowerment was coded and too distant, leaving us with only art and nostalgia. Where are we going? Where have we been? "OM GATE GATE PARAGATE PARASAM GATE . . ." Beyond the beyond.

The generator sputters and coughs and the hotel lights come on. But the rest of Siem Reap is still in darkness.

Back in the room, Lynn falls into a fitful sleep while I watch the Asia news over the BBC. North Korea is building an atom bomb. The Chinese are playing hard-ball with the British over Hong Kong. The Khmer Rouge have killed another eight people near Phnom Penh. The Japanese are in an economic slump. The Australians are worried about the ozone layer thinning over Antarctica. I look at Lynn. She's staring at the ceiling. Her fever is worse, and I give her two Tylenol and wipe her brow with a damp towel. She whispers that she doesn't have the will or energy to go on. I try and help her sit up, but she's too weak. There is no phone. There is no one to ask for help. Outside, there is a curfew and the darkened streets are deserted, waiting for the Khmer

Rouge. She moans. She can't fight anymore, she whispers. She can't stop thinking of Ayrev. She wants to be with him. Where is he? Where has he gone? I bend closer. "I understand about Peter and Robert." (Her two closest friends, Peter Hujar and Robert Mapplethorpe, who both died of AIDS.) "How they couldn't fight anymore. How they came to a point where they had to let go. I want to let go. I'm so weak."

I wrap her body in mine. "You can't let go," I whisper. "It's not part of the brochure. Anyway, what would I do without you? I barely know how to boil water."

She smiles weakly, closing her eyes. Is this really happening? Is she really going to die in Cambodia? I can't accept that.

I wipe her entire body with the damp towel. I won't let it happen. It will not happen. In a mad profane moment I wonder whom I will call if she dies. Do I call my lawyer? My agent? A friend? Is there a lama I can call? A healer? Can I call Gelek Rinpoche, who helped us so much when Ayrev died? What could he say that he didn't say before? What can anyone say? There is no one to call. For one thing, there isn't a phone. No help. No doctor. No witness. We are totally alone. Or she is alone. I am with her, but she is slipping into a solitude where I am unable to follow her. I pull myself up, holding her hand, sitting on the edge of the bed. Just be with her. Be with her breathing, let go of your mind. If you're going to dial someone, dial yourself.

And don't freak out if you reach a busy signal. Just hold her. I think of the *bardo* prayers that are forever engraved in my mind, prayers that we said every morning and evening for months, for Ayrev, for ourselves, for all those countless beings who have died and are dying and will die:

> O Buddhas and Bodhisattvas, you possess understanding wisdom, loving compassion, effective action, and protecting power beyond the reach of thought. O Compassionate Ones, *someone* is going from this world to the other shore. . . .

I can't say her name. I can't say *Lynn,* as if that would make it happen. I can only say *someone, anyone.* But not her. Not Lynn. The words continue, as if by themselves:

> Someone is leaving this world, someone is dying without choice, someone has no friends, is suffering greatly, has no refuge, has no protector, has no allies . . . (who? who? who?) . . . the light of this life has set, someone is going to another world . . . (No one. No one. No one). But someone somewhere is entering a great wilderness, is swept away by a great ocean, is going where there is no solid ground . . . Someone is terrified by the Messen-

gers of the Lord of Death . . . Lynn, myself, everyone,
are helpless . . . O Compassionate Ones, be a refuge to
Lynn Davis, who has no refuge, protect her, defend her,
keep her from the great darkness of the *bardo*. . . .

I can't go on. I just sit on the side of the bed. No
prayers. No thoughts. No hope. Why can't I move? Why
can't I find myself? Lynn is somewhere between waking
and sleeping. She is strangely calm. Several times she
looks at me, trying with her eyes to reassure me, which
makes me even more alarmed.

Finally, the first light of dawn filters into the room.
The long night is over. She is still alive. She is even
able to sit up and get dressed.

While we can still move, we decide to get on the next
plane to Phnom Penh.

* * *

The waiting room at the airport is full of armed UN
troops. We sit without talking. The room is a halfway
station. A *bardo* passage, which is where we started this
voyage in the Bangkok airport. Our pilgrimage is over.
But we have not yet been delivered back to anything
resembling a life that we can recognize. Finally we
board a plane. Somehow we survive the hour flight back
to Phnom Penh.

> Not to be reached by (merely) traveling is World's End
>> ever:
> Yet there is no release from grief unless World's End
>> be reached.
> So let a man become world-knower, wise, world-ender,
> Let him have led the holy life
> Knowing World's End, as one who is quenched, he
>> longs not for this world or another.
>
> —*Samyutta Nikaya*

In Phnom Penh we decide to continue on to Bangkok, where we know we can get to a doctor. If we stay here, we might find ourselves in the middle of a civil war, which seems ready to break out at any moment.

Our plane won't leave for another three hours. To fill the time, we go back to the Cambodiana to pick up several Dharma books I had forgotten to pack.

At an intersection, our taxi slows, passing a body lying twisted in a pool of blood near an overturned truck and a totally demolished car. Was it a bomb or an accident? A flashbulb memory: Ayrev lying on the gurney in the Phoenix hospital. Lynn touching his brow, kissing his eyes, lifting up the sheet covering his body, standing absolutely still, outside of time, as she stares at the death of her son.

The books are not at the hotel. Perhaps it is time to give up these Dharma quotations that have surrounded me on this trip like a security blanket, reminding me of the endless subjectivity of a mind that jumps through its habitual hoops like a rat in a cage.

In any case, our pilgrimage, if this is what this journey has been, is over. We have coffee in the lobby of the hotel. Somehow we both know that we will survive the exhaustion of our own personal tragedy and go on. With less hope and with less fear. Perhaps with even a larger acceptance of the inevitability of suffering and of joy as well. And perhaps, also, there will be different priorities in our daily lives; beyond the usual distractions, beyond entertainment, beyond the material, beyond the sick addictions of our own culture. We ask ourselves what will replace these old descriptions. Will we fall back into our own mechanical rhythms, our own ignorant projections? Probably. No doubt. But it will somehow be different.

As we ride back to the airport, we confront an enormous traffic jam at the scene of the accident. UN troops are everywhere. A dozen soldiers try to direct traffic, but the only machines moving are the bicycles and motorcycles which zip around the congestion like hysterical waterbugs. We only have half an hour until our plane leaves, and we are suddenly, totally panicked. Everything depends on making this flight. All our hopes and fears are crystallized toward this one goal. As quickly as we had congratulated ourselves for what we learned on this journey, we have forgotten. Forgotten mindfulness. Forgotten the action of nonaction. Forgotten "neither coming nor going." Forgotten the illuminated stares of the Buddhas of Angkor Thom and the sweet swaying step of the walking Buddha in Sukhothai proceeding toward His own becoming.

The driver shrugs, saying that our only chance is a motorcycle. We stagger out of the taxi with our bags. The driver waves down two motorcycles, telling the drivers, both teenage boys wearing Adidas and Guns n' Roses T-shirts, that we have ten minutes to make a plane.

Holding our bags clutched in our arms, we climb on back of the motorcycles. The drivers grin maniacally at each other, then Lynn's driver kick-starts his machine, and she disappears down the jammed chaotic street. As my motorcycle coughs into life, I can see her silver curtain of hair streaming out behind her like a diaphanous halo. And then she is gone. Perhaps I will never see her again. Images of the fall of Phnom Penh and Saigon flood over me . . . of refugees everywhere fleeing from disasters beyond comprehension, without portfolios, without destinations. A wave of homeless washing across the earth. And then, for a moment, I let go. No more Lynn, no more Ayrev, no more grief, no more fear, no more hope, no more happiness, no more suffering.

No more letting go. There is just the wind and the shifting, leaning exhilaration of the motorcycle as it maneuvers past obstacle after obstacle looming up on all sides of us, life arising and passing and arising once again.

*   *   *

We arrive at the airport as the gate closes. We are the last travelers they let through.

> This existence of ours is as transient as autumn clouds.
> To watch the birth and death of beings is like looking at
>   the movements of a dance.
> A lifetime is like a flash of lightning in the sky.
> Rushing by, like a torrent down a steep mountain.
> —*Diamond Sutra*